7 Memories: Partnering to Write a Memoir

Guide and Templates

<u>NEW</u>: Adaptations for Dementia

IT'S ABOUT TIME

Patricia Benesh Ed.D

"Memoir partnering brings me back to the world. It's fun to talk about and realize the blessings I have."
BJ, 97- year-old partner with Trish.

"My mom and I love doing this. From the beginning, I had a sense of relief knowing where to start. The questions are awesome. The prompts make a world of difference as they bring out information I hadn't thought about. And I'm learning things about my mom I never knew. This method has been a gift to both of us."
Rosemary with her 86-year-old mom.

"My dad didn't like to talk much about himself. When I got him focused on photos and memorabilia, it opened a new world of discussion. He realized the many successes he had and we laughed a lot. The Memoir Partnering Method brought us much closer together." **Mark with his 91-year-old dad.**

"I am honestly touched by this intergenerational oral history project wherein Trish taught us how to make a memoir with an older adult, our Exceptional Person (EP). The reminiscing led to the creation of the memoirs and a deeper understanding of the EPs and a benefit for the EPs themselves. As several students said, their EPs were very enthusiastic and joyful about having a memoir created for them. This intergenerational oral history project was a success at every angle." **Student, UCSD Life Course Scholars program**

7Memories.com a division of AuthorAssist.com
http://7Memories.com
Quantity sales. Special discounts are available on quantity purchases by corporations, associations, and others. For details, e-mail: Info@7Memories.com.

Patricia Benesh—2nd ed.
ISBN: 978-0-9986818-3-2

Table of Contents

Outline of Contents

In memory of an Extraordinary Person, Betty Jo Strong

Reading my memoir is like calling up an old friend.

Betty Jo Strong (1919-2018)

.

OVERVIEW

The Memoir Partnering Method

- Have you ever been with a friend or family member and noticed that his or her memory seemed to be fading—and had that feeling of urgency to capture some significant memories?

- Have you ever been curious about the life of another person and wished you knew more about him or her?

- Have you ever lost someone before you had a chance to capture some of his or her memories?

- Have your children ever been curious to know more about their grandparents, but you have little information to offer?

- Do you wish there was an easy way to start a conversation and capture memories that can become a treasured legacy for future generations?

If you answered yes to any of the above, you are the perfect candidate for the Memoir Partnering Method. You have the potential to be an invaluable memoir partner by bonding with and collecting memories of this person—your extraordinary person.

What's New in this Second Edition?

In the past several years, *7 Memories: Partnering to Write a Memoir* has been adapted by volunteers, family members, and caregivers for use with early-stage and middle-stage dementia patients. The adaptations are described and included in this second edition as follows:

- Differences regarding normal memory loss, early-stage dementia, and mid-stage dementia

- Reminiscence Therapy as the foundation of the Memoir Partnering Method

- Importance of language and reading in communication

- Appendix B—The Mini-Memoir for Early-stage Dementia

- Appendix C—Memoir Moments for Middle-stage Dementia

The Memoir Partner (MP) and Extraordinary Person (EP)

You are the memoir partner (MP) with the sacred gift of helping create a memoir—affirming that your extraordinary person's life counts. Even if you know nothing about writing a memoir, you have everything you need to create a heartwarming memoir using the guide and templates. Whether you are a family member, friend, caregiver, or volunteer, you are a partner who believes in this method of preserving memories in the form of a written memoir, mini-memoir, or memoir moment.

Your extraordinary person may seem ordinary to the outside world, but you know the truth. The truth is that this person is extraordinary in many ways. And you want the world to know it. **For this reason, we're naming her/him an extraordinary person or EP.**

As the MP, you intend to capture some memories to help your EP write a memoir, mini-memoir, or memoir moment so as to leave a treasured legacy for generations to come. Together, you and your EP delve into memories and ideas that neither of you would experience alone. **You are embarking on this journey together through the past to create a memoir that shows a high regard for his/her life.**

The standard Memoir Partnering Method covers a manageable slice of life—just $7^{+/-}$ memories—starting with a sample session of one photo or memorabilia item. The sample session introduces your EP to the method and gets you both comfortable in the conversation. The finished memoir has 3-7 memories that reflect your EP's hopes and dreams, awesome experiences, and personality. **The memories may span the lifetime or focus on a specific topic. The memoir does not have to be chronological. Most important is the message your EP wants to convey. The result is your EP's unique memoir.** Your gift of time and caring in this process is invaluable—and makes the memoir a reality for your EP.

Adapting the Partnering Method to Memory Loss and Dementia

You may notice that your EP is challenged at times with memory recall. Or you may know or suspect that your EP has some level of dementia. What to do? Choose one of the adaptations as follows.

Realize, as our population ages, the issue of memory loss and dementia increases. While there are numerous scales and definitions of memory loss and dementia, the purpose here is to offer some general descriptions, so you can adapt the Memoir Partnering Method accordingly. In the case where dementia is known (or suspected), you will want to discuss the matter with the appropriate loved one or care-giver. You will find that the Reflective Listening Technique (Appendix D) and your patience and consideration go a long way toward successful partnering with your EP no matter where s/he may fall on the memory scale.

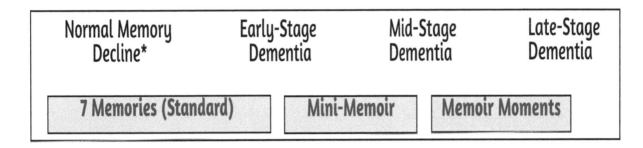

Normal Memory Decline includes minor problems with memory, speech, or decision-making that do not notably interfere with activities of daily life. According to research, some form of memory loss is experienced by nearly 40 percent of people over the age of 65. As long as there is no underlying medical condition causing it, this type of memory loss is considered a normal part of the aging.

*Normal memory loss does not necessarily progress to dementia. The standard Memoir Partnering Method is ideal for older adults with normal memory loss.

Early-stage dementia is indicated when persons have difficulty with Activities of Daily Living (ADLs) such as managing finances, driving, grocery shopping, meal preparation, home maintenance, and medications. There is increased forgetfulness along with difficulty finding the right words and concentrating. The cognitive decline is noticeable to loved ones.

As this stage progresses, there is decreased memory of recent events and greater difficulty with ADLs. The person may be in denial of the symptoms and start to withdraw from family and friends as socialization becomes more difficult. The cognitive decline can be verified using standard dementia-related interviews and exams.

Depending on the extent of memory loss and concentration, the Memoir Partnering Method for Early-Stage dementia can be:

- used in the standard manner as described throughout the book.

- limited to shorter sessions and fewer memories (for example, eliminate Step 3 and omit optional homework).

- adapted using the Mini-Memoir (Appendix B).

Middle-stage dementia shows significant memory loss that may affect major aspects of life, such as remembering current address, phone number, date, year, or where they are. Assistance is needed in completing some ADLs such as dressing, bathing or preparing meals. The person may be at home with help from a loved one and caregivers or in a care facility. At this stage, the MP can choose to adapt using:

- the Mini-Memoir (Appendix B) or

- Memoir Moments (Appendix C)

Be sure to shorten the sessions as your EP tires or loses concentration.

Late-stage Dementia reveals the need for extensive assistance to carry out ADLs. This stage is marked by forgetting names of close family members and having little memory of recent events, and perhaps remembering only some details of earlier life. There may be difficulty counting down from 10 and finishing tasks. Incontinence and personality changes may occur. The dementia may deteriorate to the point of an inability to speak or communicate and the need for assistance with most activities.

Some specific aspects of Memoir Moments may be appropriate at this late-stage of dementia. Certainly activities such as, reminiscing, watching old movies, singing familiar songs, and reading aloud may be pleasant for an EP at this stage.

As the chart on the next page shows, the three Memoir Partnering approaches have the critical components to stimulate mental activity and memory using: Reminiscence Therapy with photos, memorabilia, and activities; Reflective Listening; prompts to start conversations; flexible sessions for memoir-making; optional homework; and optional use of technology.

Major differences are shown for tailoring the Memoir Partnering Method to the skill of your EP—basically, the number and length of sessions, the optional homework, and the use of technology. The resulting memoir may be a full-fledged memoir book, a shorter mini-memoir, or memoir moments as pages, notecards, or flashcards. There is no fixed criteria for using one approach over another. As the MP, you decide which of the three approaches is best suited to the abilities of your EP. Thus, you will want to be familiar with the three approaches so you can "borrow" ideas from one approach or another to tailor it for your EP.

Memoir Partnering Method: 3 Approaches Adapted to Memory

Normal Memory Decline*	Early-Stage Dementia	Mid-Stage Dementia	Late-Stage Dementia
7 Memories (Standard)		Mini-Memoir	Memoir Moments

	7 MEMORIES (Standard)	MINI-MEMOIR (Appendix B)	MEMOIR MOMENTS (Appendix C)
Use of Photos, Memorabilia, and Activities to Spark Memory	✓	✓	✓
Reminiscence Therapy	✓	✓	✓
Reflective Listening	✓	✓	✓
Provides Prompts to Engage in Conversation	200+ Prompts in 18 categories	20 Prompts and Others as Appropriate	Numerous General Prompts
Flexible Number and Length of Sessions	12 +/-	6 +/-	1 +
Creates Custom Reading and Memory Materials	Memoir Book of Any Length	Shorter Memoir Book	Memoir Pages or Flashcards
Examples	✓	✓	✓
Templates	✓		
Optional Homework	✓	✓	✓
Optional Use of Technology	✓	✓	✓

*NOTE: Normal memory decline does not necessarily progress to dementia. See previous definitions.

Reminiscence Therapy in Partnering to Write a Memoir

Behind any physical or mental decline in an older adult, is a lifetime of precious experiences. Each person is a living history book with wonderful stories to tell of a culture that often is lost to us. When we take the time to listen with interest, reflect with them, and write their stories, we learn wonderful information about the world—and bond with them in ways we never imagined. And they benefit with improved recall and self-esteem—and a memoir ensuring they will be remembered. All of these amazing stories are lost to us and future generations, unless we take the time to encourage and help older adults reminisce and write their stories.

The Memoir Partnering Method is based on the concept of Reminiscence Therapy to create custom memoirs. As defined by the American Psychological Association, Reminiscence Therapy is the use of life histories to improve psychological well-being. The original idea is credited to Erik Erikson who included it as part of his eight stages of psychosocial development from birth to death. In late adulthood, the last stage, he posited that it becomes important for us to look back on our lives with satisfaction before we die. In 1963, Dr. Robert Butler formalized the idea and coined the term "Reminiscence Therapy."

Since the 1960s, numerous studies with older adults show that Reminiscence Therapy improves cognitive function, quality of life, and emotional well-being. It provides older adults with a sense of overall life satisfaction and coping skills, and may help to ameliorate the symptoms of depression and dementia.

Rather than approach reminiscence as therapy, we at 7 Memories approach it as intentional storytelling from one person to another, resulting in a written memoir. When the EP recalls the life-shaping challenges s/he has overcome, self-esteem, coping skills, memory, and mental agility improve. The EP reflects on life and how s/he wants to be remembered—and leaves a message. **The memoir is information passed from one generation to another—and a physical manifestation of a life that will not be forgotten.**

It's about time. *A memoir is a lifetime of experience and learning passed on to future generations. Otherwise, it's a lifetime lost, like a library burning to the ground.*

The Role of Language in Communication

The role of language in communication cannot be understated.

> "Language is not only a vehicle for the expression of thoughts, perceptions, sentiments, and values characteristic of a community; it also represents a fundamental expression of social identity."
> (Edward Sapir)

> Language shapes thoughts and emotions, determining one's perception of reality.
> (Benjamin Whorf)

In human development, language starts with hearing in the womb at about 25-26 weeks. The most significant sound the fetus hears in the womb is the mother's voice. In the third trimester, the fetus can already recognize it.

On the language development spectrum, hearing develops to listening, then to speaking, then to reading and then to writing. So the spectrum looks like this:

Hearing ----→ Listening -----→ Speaking ----→ Reading ----→ Writing

In memory loss, we may see communication skills decline, with writing, reading, and speaking skills often deteriorating in the reverse order. Because these skills are critical to the ability to communicate, the Memoir Partnering Method focuses on reinforcing these skills.

The Memoir Partnering Method addresses the entire language spectrum and provides opportunities for reinforcement through the partnering sessions and the optional homework. The optional homework involves writing and reading to the extent possible—using the material created during the partnering session. **As the MP, be aware of your EP's communication ability and encourage your EP to use these communication skills daily.**

If reading is beyond your EP's ability, read aloud or use text-to-speech technology so your EP can listen to the material. Be sure to explore the many helpful technological aides accessible in smart phones, tablets, and computers for use with your EP.

The Special Role of Reading in the Partnering Method

Reading is an automatic response over a lifetime. It's so ingrained in us from an early age, we are not even aware that we are reading signs, posters, billboards, etc. Reading stimulates mental activity, forges new pathways in the brain, and improves memory.

The problem is that there are few appropriate reading materials for those whose memory is fading. Large print books and magazines are too complicated with too many photos and complex content. They provide no focus and can be confusing. On the other hand, children's books have simple pictures and content, but they are not appropriate for adults.

As the MP, you are creating custom reading material perfectly tailored to your EP since it is developed from his/her photos, memorabilia, or daily activities. The memoir can be in the form of a page collected in a binder or loose leaf notebook.--or notecards (like flashcards) stored in a file box.

My three siblings: Rosie, Katie, Me, and Izzie

Sample Notecard from a Memoir Moment (Appendix C)

Leave a copy of the session narrative for your EP. It is important that you leave a copy of your written narrative with your EP-- either that day or at the following session. Encourage her or him to read it every day. Perhaps your EP can write more or add more photos or memorabilia. If s/he cannot read, use text-to-speech technology to provide opportunities to listen to the material. In these ways, s/he is being mentally stimulated while reinforcing communication skills.

Birds-eye View of the Standard Memoir Partnering Method

The memoir is created over a series of 8-12 sessions* of 30-60 minutes duration. Each memoir session involves five steps, based on a photo/memorabilia: 1) conversation, reflective listening, and questions, 2) note-taking and photographing the item, 3) providing optional EP "homework" as appropriate, 4) creating a draft page from the notes and photo, and 5) prepping for the next session. The guide includes instructions for each step and accompanying templates for you and your EP.

First, offer an invitation, by phone or in person, to your potential partner and ask permission.

- Invite your EP on this journey to the past with you—to create a memoir together of 3-7 memories in a series of 30–60-minute conversations over 8-12 sessions.
- Start the invitation by relating what you want to do—and why you want to do it.
- Explain that you start with a sample session that introduces the method and offers the opportunity for feedback, including whether or not the EP wants to continue.
- Agree on a time and place for the sample session.
- Be sure to ask permission from others who may be involved peripherally, such as spouses, partners, roommates, caregivers, etc.
- Exchange contact information with your EP and remind your EP of your appointment a day prior.
- **Ask your EP to choose one photo or memorabilia for the session and make some notes about the item.** This will allow your EP to think ahead about the importance of the item.
- If your EP has difficulty choosing an item, help by identifying something in the room or that s/he is wearing that may be significant. Or use What's in a Name? (Appendix C) for the sample session.

Session 1 (Sample): Engage in a Sample Memory.
- Show the sample memoir (Alice Fern, Appendix J)
- Use the Sample Session templates to focus on the one chosen photo or memorabilia item.
- Help your EP if s/he has difficulty choosing an item by choosing something notable. Or use Memoir Moments (Appendix C) as this may be the most you can do with your EP at this time.
- Engage in the method: a conversation of listening, asking questions, and note-taking.
- Take a photo of the chosen photo/memorabilia for use in the next session. Or take a selfie of the two of you together.
- Get feedback on the session and determine if your EP wants to continue.
- If yes, use the Agreement Template to establish a set day/time/place to meet, and the number of photos/memorabilia to include (3-7).
- If appropriate, offer the optional homework template for independent follow-up.

Session 2: Create a Draft Cover Page, Message, and List of 3-7 Items.
- Use the Session 2 templates and the photo from the sample session to create the draft title page. This motivates your EP and helps you begin the conversation about the message your EP wants the memoir to convey. What does your EP want readers to remember from the memoir?
- List your EP's 3-7 memories and make sure the memories and message are in sync.
- Discuss additional photos and memorabilia your EP wants to include such as: significant events, important people in his/her life, or focusing on a single, significant topic. In any case, you want to keep the process reasonable and finish the memoir in 8-12 sessions. You can always add more later.
- Offer the optional homework template for independent follow-up.

Session 3: Refine and Sequence the Items (Option to omit or use in a later session.)
- Use the Session 3 templates for your EP to mull over the items and make changes until s/he is satisfied in knowing that each photo/memorabilia is in sync with the overall message. These items create the framework of the memoir.
- Complete the summary sheet for reference.
- Offer the optional homework template for independent follow-up.

Sessions 4-9: Create the Next Memories Using the Templates
- Use the same method as in the sample session, starting with reflective listening and baseline questions to get first thoughts.
- Continue with questions and note-taking to add details and depth.
- Use the memory prompts in Appendix H as needed.
- Offer the optiona lhomework templates for independent follow-up.

Check-up Session
- Provide a print copy of the memoir pages for review by your EP.
- Use the 14-item check-up template to determine the changes needed for the final draft.
- Offer the optional template for independent follow-up.

Review Session: The Final Draft.
- Consider the final draft title, cover photo, dedication and memoir pages with your EP and the changes needed for the finished version.
- Ask your EP to consider the various options for printing and distributing the memoir.
- Discuss how your EP would like to spend the last session.
- Offer the optional homework template for independent follow-up.

Last Session: The Finished Memoir.
- Provide the proofread final version of the memoir in print and digital file format.
- Read it together and discuss methods of sharing the memoir and names of friends/family for distribution.
- Ask your EP for feedback about the memoir partnering experience.

*Note: Use the Mini-Memoir (Appendix B) to shorten the method to 6+/- sessions if your EP cannot participate in the standard Memoir Partnering Method. Or you may find Memoir Moments (Appendix C) more appropriate for your EP.

See the Standard Session Chart on the next page for the focus, TO-Dos, templates, and optional EP homework.

Session Chart for 7 Memories Standard Approach

SESSION	FOCUS	TO-DO	TEMPLATES	OPTIONAL EP HOMEWORK
INVITATION TO YOUR EP	Introductory material	-Explain partnering method to your EP -Schedule sample session -EP chooses 1 item for sample session		Choose 1 item for the sample session
SESSION 1 (SAMPLE) Memory #1	1 photo or memorabilia item	-Show Alice Fern memoir -Use sample templates -Complete agreement	-Alice Fern -Note-taking -Agreement -EP homework -Finished page	Read Alice Fern Memoir List 7+ items for the memoir
SESSION 2	Cover page Item list Memoir message	-Read 1st memory -Complete cover page -List 7 memorabilia -Write memoir message	-Cover page -Item list -Memoir message -EP homework	List additional memorabilia Write importance of memorabilia
SESSION 3 (OPTIONAL)	Refine items Refine sequence	-Refine item list -Sequence items -Summarize	-Refine item list -Sequence items -Summary Sheet -EP homework	List additional important items
SESSIONS 4-9 Memories 2-7	1 photo or memorabilia item per session	-Questions and note taking for each item -Read and refine memory at next session	For each item: -Note-taking -EP homework -Finished pages	Read and review current memory Add zest to current memory
CHECK-UP SESSION	14-Item check-up	-Show draft memoir -Review with 14-item check-up	14 Questions for Check-up	Read and review draft for further changes
NEXT-TO-LAST SESSION	Final draft memoir	-Review final draft to make changes	Final draft memoir pages	-Read final draft -List memoir recipients
LAST SESSION	Final Draft	Read and Celebrate		Distribute

Using the Templates

The templates included in this guide are for you and your EP. Directions for your note-taking and draft templates are in small print. Directions for your EP are in large print. The template pages can be copied and printed for pen/pencil completion with your EP during each session.

The Digital Templates:

- Download the free digital templates document file from Info@7Memories.com. The templates document file will allow you to enter your work digitally on your computer. (If it opens in "read only mode," be sure to click and use it in "edit mode" or save it with another name.)
  - Enter and edit each memory, then copy/paste each final page to the final template file for the finished version.
  - Or work directly in the final template and update as you add and edit the memoir.
  - Consider using font for large print 14-18 pt. for the memoir.

Alternatively: Use your own word document software to generate the memoir pages.

Use Technology: If you hate to type, consider using speech-to-text software. Most computers, tablets, and cell phones have them installed as standard software. There are numerous free versions of commercial programs, such as Dragon and Speechnotes. Speech-to-text software has come a long way and can be remarkably accurate.

Tailoring the Standard Memoir Partnering Method for Your EP:

- Modify the session length and prompts to suit your EP's interests and capabilities:
  - Shorten by modifying Session 2 and/or Session 3.
  - Sequence the sessions as needed, for example, create the cover page in a later session.
  - Shorten by omitting Session 3.
  - Use the Mini-Memoir (Appendix B) or Memoir Moments (Appendix C)
- Lengthen by adding more sessions.
- Use an associated item from a photo album, collection, or a relevant item from a magazine or stock photo gallery if your EP includes memories without photos/memorabilia.
- Be sure to capture stories your EP repeats in casual conversation. Get the details with the *who, what, when, where, how, and why* questions and add others from the prompts in Appendix H.
- Use the appropriate font size: 16pt; 18pt or larger if needed by your EP.

Adapting the Method for Long Distance EPs

Use the phone or video chatting such as Facetime or Skype. This can work for the initial invitation, scheduling of sessions, and subsequent conversations if your EP lives too distant for face-to-face conversations. Take notes and/or record the conversations using the templates as usual. If your EP uses e-mail, all the better for collecting photos and providing copies of finished sessions.

At the start, collect 7+ photos for inclusion in the memoir. It's a good idea to collect all 7+ photos before you begin the process so you're ready to proceed without interruption. **Consider these various options for your EP:**

- Place the photos online using cloud storage, such as Google drive, Dropbox, etc.

- E-mail the photos to you.

- Snail mail a thumb drive or CD of the photos to you.

- Snail mail paper copies of the photos to you.

- Get help with any of the above.

Follow up each session with the memory from the previous session. If your EP uses e-mail, you can e-mail copies of the memoir sessions for review and revision. If not, read aloud the memory from the previous session over the phone/Skype to make any necessary changes. For the next-to-last session, send your EP a draft of the finished memoir by e-mail, uploading to cloud storage, or snail mailing a thumb drive, CD or paper copies.

Identify helpers your EP may need. Depending on your EPs abilities, s/he may need for help with the process, i.e. submitting the photos and maintaining the session contacts and conversations. Discuss this issue with your EP during the invitation and connect with persons who will be helping him/her. Ensure that the helper understands the process and is committed to pitch in along the way.

Adapting the Method for Activity Centers, Groups, Families, and Friends

Working with a group: Provide EPs with handouts of the templates to complete independently with pen or pencil. Rotate among EPs to offer individual help. Ideally, EPs would dictate into a computer using standard speech-to-text software on most computers. That eliminates the need for transcription.

Working with pairs in a group: EPs work in pairs, alternating between being the interviewer and the interviewee. Provide EPs with handouts of the templates to complete with pen or pencil. Rotate among the pairs to offer help. Ideally, EPs will dictate into a computer using standard speech-to-text software on most computers. That eliminates the need for transcription.

Taking turns in a small group: Have one EP relate a story of his/her photo or memento recorded by a staff member or volunteer. At the next session, the EP or staff member/volunteer reads it to the group to determine if any changes are needed. Then the next EP in the group takes a turn relating a memory as recorded by a staff member or volunteer … and so forth. This works well if the number of sessions per week matches the number of EPs in the group. For example, if the group meets five days a week with five EPs, each EP takes a turn once a week to create his/her own memory page.

Using staff members or volunteers: Train staff, interns, volunteers, college students, or community service high school students to use the Memoir Partnering Method. Family members and friends can learn too.

Alternating among family members: The Memoir Partnering Method is a perfect family activity whereby each member commits to creating one or more memoir pages with the EP. Identify one family member to take the lead in scheduling the sessions, collecting the pages, and putting together the final version. Then celebrate together with family members as you present the finished memoir. Imagine how much love your EP feels given this caring attention.

Alternating with friends or siblings: Two or more friends or siblings can work together to create their memoirs, sharing in their memories. Imagine getting to know a friend at this deeper level. Or invite more friends and create a memoir-writing circle to write and share memories.

Creating a library of memoirs: Include copies of these memoirs in the library so they can be shared with others and used for motivational purposes.

Finding an MP for an EP

You may know an EP, or you may be an EP yourself, in need of an MP. The EP may have recently moved to the residence or have had family and friends move away. In this ever-changing world, EP's may find themselves without local family or close friends to partner in creating a memoir.

Friends, caregivers, and volunteers are perfect potential MPs. In choosing an MP, make sure s/he is:

- friendly and will create a comfortable atmosphere for conversation and memoir-making.

- trustworthy in keeping confidences.

- responsible and will commit to the time and schedule for completing the memoir.

- light-hearted and likes to laugh.

- a believer in the Memoir Partnering Method and the legacy being created together. Alternatively, consider asking a friend or relative to try it on a long distance basis with you. (See the section *Adapting the Method for Long Distance.)*

YOUR GIFT

You as the Memoir Partner

As the memoir partner, your time is a precious gift for your EP and for all who will read and cherish the memoir. Without your efforts, the experiences and values of your EP would be lost forever—like a library burning to the ground.

Your EP may have thought about writing a memoir, but never got around to it, or tried and never finished, or felt that no one would be interested or care to know. But you realize there's a lifetime of your EP's hopes and dreams, her/his strong personality traits, and awesome experiences to be remembered. They form the message about your EP's life and unique essence.

Now your EP has the time, but maybe not the inclination to write a memoir. That's where you come in as—the explorer—helping your EP delve into the past and writing down memories to leave a treasured legacy. **Realize, it's not an autobiography or a blow-by-blow account of your EP's life. In the standard approach, the memoir focuses on a series of moments around a theme.** In this case, you'll introduce the method with one memory; then move toward capturing 3-7 memories.

The Benefits of Writing a Memoir

There are many personal reasons for helping your EP write a memoir, mini-memoir, or memoir moment including a multitude of benefits to you and your EP. It allows you and your EP to leave a gift of kindness and caring—imparting experiences and values to future generations. It's holding up a mirror to your EP's life—and showing that it counts.

The 7 benefits to your EP of writing a memoir:

1. **Improves memory and mental agility.** It's a challenging activity that sparks old and new memories. Science has proven the plasticity of the brain so these mental activities may lead to generating new brain cells.

2. **Teaches new skills.** Specifically, how to organize and write his/her thoughts–and how to inform and entertain others.

3. **Encourages connections with others—even those your EP may have lost touch with years ago.** It allows a safe place for offering information your EP may not have been willing to share previously. It fosters the healing of old wounds, thus forging a path to forgiveness. And it can lead to your EP reuniting with former family and friends through e-mail and social media.

4. **Sparks curiosity about your EP among his/her family and friends.** They'll marvel at your EP's story and want to know more. It may motivate others to research details or to start journaling, or even to write their own memoirs.

5. **Leads to a better understanding of oneself**. The method results in a deeper insight of your EP's significant life events. It shows how your EP thinks and offers a place to express his/her uniqueness. This leads to self-awareness and self-acceptance.

6. **Leads to a greater realization of your EP's personal power**. Remembering how s/he dealt with struggles and overcame obstacles can lead to greater current strength and resilience. It's holding up a mirror to your EP's life—and showing that it counts.

7. **Offers the opportunity to honor others in your EP's life**. Remembering and showing appreciation to those who have nurtured and supported his/her dreams leaves a lasting impression about your EP.

The 7 benefits of reading your EP's memoir:

1. Offers a message to future generations.
2. Teaches positive values from the past.
3. Helps others understand the importance of their legacy and the effects of significant life events.
4. Sparks an interest in doing ancestral research and writing a journal or memoir.
5. Provides a legacy—a gift of kindness and caring from one generation to another
6. Leads to deeper connections, healing, and forgiveness.
7. Honors those of the past.

As the memoir partner, you:

1. Learn powerful listening skills.
2. Learn basic story-writing and memoir-writing skills.
3. Learn tactful interviewing skills.
4. Learn proven proofreading skills.
5. Make a deep significant connection with your EP and others.
6. Enhance EP self-esteem by honoring his/her life.
7. Help create a legacy for future generations.

Your Intentions as the Memoir Partner

- Why are you helping your EP write a memoir? What is the most important benefit to you?

- What makes this person an EP? What are his/her strengths?

- What makes you think your EP is open to this idea?

- What doubts might your EP have and how can you help overcome them?

Share your reasons with your EP when you offer the invitation to create a memoir together.

GETTING STARTED WITH INTENTION:

Since you're reading this guide, your intention is to help produce a memoir for your EP's family and friends. Be intentional about the schedule you set—and stick to it. Choose a time when you both can be quiet and generate thoughts, when your EP feels fresh and ready to go—when your EP has time to himself/herself.

This is an ideal time for the mirror test. The mirror doesn't lie. State your intentions in front of a mirror. Look into your eyes and state your intention to help your EP write his/her memoir.

Right NOW: Stand in front of a mirror and reaffirm your goal: *"I am sticking to my goal to help my EP write his/her memoir."*

HINT: Set alarms to remind you and your EP of the schedule.

BE SURE TO:

- **Read the Overview and Your Gift chapters.** It's background information, the foundation of the Memoir Partnering Method, and it sets the stage for the invitation and sample sessions.
- Provide your EP a file folder or binder to organize and keep the draft memoir pages.
- Organize your MP documents in a file folder, binder, and/or computer file.
- **Remember where the EP and MP files are kept.**

THE EP INTRODUCTION

The Invitation

Invite your EP to engage in the Memoir Partnering Method. Explain why you want to do it and the benefits to future generations and to the EP himself/herself. The invitation may be best face-to-face or by phone depending on the particular situation. Your goal is to have your EP agree to the sample session—to try out the Memoir Partner Method.

Explaining the Method

- The method is a series of conversations about selected photos/memorabilia to evoke memories. Items include photos, scrapbooks, diaries, journals, collections, awards, medals, certificates, letters, e-mail, blogs, speeches, poems, artwork, etc. You'll start with 3-7 photos/memorabilia items.

- Ideally, the selected items will be significant and thematic, focusing on a specific topic such as important people; military experiences, raising children, travels, hobbies, etc. Remember, this is not an autobiography and it does not have to be written in chronological order. The theme or message is of greatest importance.

- Each session will take 30-60 minutes and will be scheduled at a mutually convenient time/place. The overall project will take 8-12 sessions or less depending on the chosen number of memorabilia and your EP's level.

- You will record/take notes during each session and ask questions to add details and depth. The resulting memoir will be a document that can be distributed to friends and family.

- You'll begin with a sample session, after which your EP can decide to engage in the method—or not.

- It's an open-ended method that continues until the selected memories are finished and the memoir is ready to print and distribute. The EP determines the end point and can stop at any time.

Discussing the Time and Place for the Sample Session

- Choose a time when your EP and you can be quiet and generate thoughts, when your EP feels fresh, and ready to go—and when your EP has time to himself/herself.

- Discuss the best place conducive to conversing and writing—one that will evoke memories and inspire your EP to write about them. Hopefully, your EP will want to meet in his/her abode—that's where s/he feels most at ease. Regardless of the place, consider a comfy, quiet room away from distractions such as other people, TVs, cell phones, games, and hobbies.

- Explain that you will provide a reminder a day prior to your meeting.

- Exchange contact information for communications and determine the best way to contact your EP: phone, e-mail, text, etc.

- Discuss that you'll be arriving with your "tools" such as digital recorder, cell phone, pencil/paper, notebook, computer/tablet, etc. Discuss the need to record the session, take notes, and photograph the memorabilia using your tools.

- **Ask your EP to be ready with some of his/her photos and memorabilia. Help identify what to include. Be prepared to take photos.**

- **If your EP cannot decide, take the lead. Look around the room at photos, collections, books, journals, clothing, furniture, and focus on something interesting that strikes you for starting the conversation. Or get started with "What's in a Name?" in Appendix C.**

- Determine other persons who may be peripherally involved such as spouses, significant others, roommates, caretakers, etc. and ask permissions as appropriate.

- Put the date/time/place for the sample session on your EP's calendar. Leave your card with the date/time/place on the back, much the same as a doctor/dentist appointment—but a lot more fun.

Handling Your EP's Doubts with Affirmations

Your EP may have doubts that s/he can do this: it's too much work, s/he is not a good enough writer, it'll never get finished, nobody will want to read it, and s/he tried and failed at it before. These doubts may be revealed during the invitation or during any of the memoir sessions. Deal with these negative thoughts whenever they occur. Encourage your EP to give it a try—with a sample session.

List the doubts and add an affirmation for each doubt showing how each doubt can be overcome.

Doubt	Affirmation
• I haven't done anything important.	You are being modest. Our conversations will reveal you have done many important things.
• Nobody cares about this.	You family and friends care about this and will thank you for writing your memoir.

Using Motivational Activities to Limit EP Doubts

- Present the sample memoir (Alice Fern, Appendix J) as an example of the finished memoir.

- Show other sample pages (available at 7Memories.com) to reveal how the memoir is developed one memory at a time.

- Create the cover with your EP focusing on the dedication—who s/he wants most to read the memoir. Enlist these folks for support as appropriate.

- Display the cover or one of your EP's memory pages in a spot where those living with your EP can see it and show enthusiasm for the memoir.

- Ask family and friends to send messages regarding their excitement about the EP's forthcoming memoir.

- Send the draft cover page or one memory page to family members and friends so they can respond with encouraging messages.

Preparing for the Sample Session

Contact your EP with a reminder of your appointment a day prior to the sample session. Confirm that your EP has selected a photo/memorabilia item for the session.

Choose your "tools" for recording the session:

- Paper and pencil or computer/tablet for taking notes.

- Digital recorder/cell phone for audio recording of the session for transcribing later*.

- Speech-to-text software on your digital device.

- Combination of the above.

- Cell phone /tablet/camera for taking photos of photos and memorabilia.

- File folder or binder for your EP to keep draft memoir pages.

- File folder, binder, and/or computer file for your MP docs.

FOR THE SAMPLE SESSION, PRINT:

- Sample Memoir (Alice Fern, Appendix J)

- TEMPLATE NOTE-TAKING AND QUESTIONS FOR SAMPLE SESSION PAGE

- TEMPLATE: Agreement to Partner

- TEMPLATE: OPTIONAL—LIST 7 OR MORE PHOTOS/ITEMS FOR THE MEMOIR

*HINT: It's highly recommended that you make an audio recording or use text-to-speech software during the sample session to ensure you capture the narrative you desire. After that, you can decide if you need to record subesquent sessions or use text-to-speech software for note-taking. Or you may prefer to use pen/pencil for note-taking and text-to-speech for putting your notes into the draft template.

Selling It with the Sample Session

REMEMBER THE SAMPLE SESSION TEMPLATES:

- Sample Memoir

- Sample Session Note-taking

- Optional EP Homework: List 7 or more photos/items for the memoir

- Agreement To Partner

Etiquette 101

- **Arrive on time and be prepared for the session.** Bring your tools and materials.
- **Greet your EP with a smile and polite hello with enthusiasm for getting started.**
- **Show attention in your posture.** Sit forward and look at your EP. It may seem intense to you, but keep it light by laughing, crying, and asking questions as appropriate—keeping the focus on your EP.
- **Engage in reflective listening.** The most important aspect of each session is REFLECTIVE LIS-TENING. Stop your note-taking and show you're actively connecting with your EP by listening with concentration and engaging in reflective listening and feedback. **(See Appendix D)**
- **Respect silences.** Your EP may become quiet in his/her musing past events. Instinctively, you may want to fill awkward silences with questions or conversation to keep your EP from (and you) feeling uncomfortable. If you sit quietly and wait, you'll be surprised at what may come next. So be patient and respect the silence.

- **Be ever present with your EP.** Notice your EP's energy throughout the session and stop when s/he seems tired or ready to end the session. Don't overdo it—keep it fresh and exciting.
- **Thank your EP.** In giving the gift of listening and helping to write your EP's memoir, you are being entrusted with precious memories. Show your appreciation and gratitude for this trust.

REMEMBER: This is meant to be an enjoyable endeavor where your EP looks back, muses on the past, and fashions his/her thoughts and words so they will be cherished by readers. **Take your time and enjoy the method. Be aware of your EP's energy and when you see it waning, stop the session and continue it next time.**

The Conversation

Begin with your EP's chosen photo/item. If your EP needs help choosing an item, take the lead and suggest something you've noticed, such as photos, collections, unusual knickknacks, furniture, clothing, etc. to start a meaningful conversation. If all else fails, use "What's in a Name?" from Appendix C

The session begins with you listening to your EP first, then clarifying, asking questions, and paraphrasing your EP's thoughts before making notes. It's important that you listen intently first, so your EP sees that you are genuinely interested in him/her and the memories presented.

Your EP may veer off topic into other memories. This is where your discretion comes into play. You may find the evoked memories add depth to the narrative. If so, keep the conversation going. If not, gently guide your EP back to the topic. Perhaps repeat the last detail s/he gave or repeat the last topical question in order to return to the original topic. If your EP cannot remember exact dates and details, write in general terms.

Ask questions to add detail and depth in your conversation. Below is a list of basic questions. **Choose only those questions that are relevant for the chosen item.**

1. Tell me a little about this photo/item.
2. How did you come to have it? (Listen for the who, what, when, where, why, and how.)
3. What was the high point of the experience?
4. What obstacle(s) did you have to overcome?
5. How did it end?
6. What did you learn from the experience?
7. What impact did it have on you and your hopes and dreams?
8. Why is this photo/item important to you?

Practice reflective listening by summarizing or paraphrasing your EP's comments, starting with a phrase such as:

- "What I hear you saying is …"

- "It sounds like …"

- "It seems as if…."

Then take brief notes. You will organize and expand your notes later. For now:

- **Be sure to write in first person** (I, me, my, we, us, our)—as it creates the most personal and heartwarming tone.

- **Take notes of basic facts,** key words, and phrases.

- **Don't worry about spelling or writing complete grammatical sentences.** It's important just to record your EP's ideas for this memory.

Prompt Your EP to:

- **Give detailed answers to questions such as:** What did you see? Where were you? Who was with you? What happened?

- **Be prepared with other prompts by category from Appendix H.**

- **Visualize the memory to add sensory details.** If your EP closes his/her eyes, perhaps s/he can recall sensory information, such as touch, smell, taste, sight, and sound. Encourage your EP to include sizzling words and phrases that let readers imagine the color, noises, scents, flavors, and feelings.

- **Describe another person associated with the experience.** Include characteristics that are unique or quirky such as physical appearance, clothing, gait, dialect, habits, hobbies, interests, favorite sayings, books, movies, music, songs. Write in active voice showing who is doing the action, for example, "He talked with a lisp that made him sound quite funny, even when he was trying to be serious."

Add zest to the memory. Encourage your EP to offer:

- **Family sayings.** Quote those quaint phrases spoken in your EP's family day in and day out. Every family has had some original expressions, such as, "Use it up, wear it out, make it do." "Anything worth doing is worth doing well." "You can move a mountain with a teaspoon."

- **Anecdotes.** These are little stories handed down in families that can brighten a memoir and make for interesting reading. Shorten the anecdote to a few sentences and be sure to relate its importance.

- **Favorite books, music, hobbies, and special interests.** These provide great insight into your EP and the specific era of his/her life. They may motivate others to explore these details.

- **Historical highlights.** Historical events and culture shape a life and give great depth to the memoir.

- **Songs, lyrics, quotes, poems, etc** . There's a great deal of nostalgia in recalling the words of a song, quotes from a book, speech, etc. Why not quote a phrase or line to set the mood? For example, "You make me smile with my heart." from the song, "My Funny Valentine."

- **Relevant material from journals, diaries, letters, e-mail, blogs, and social networks**. These are wonderful references for remembering details, emotions, and thoughts.

- **Humor**. A dash of humor can lighten the tone and provide variety. Use it sparingly and in good taste.

Ending the Session

Stop the memoir conversation after 30-60 minutes when your EP has finished talking.

Ask for feedback from your EP.

- "How do you feel about our conversation today?"
- "What did you like about it?"
- "Is there anything you didn't like about it?"
- "How can we change it to make it better for you?"
- "Would you like to continue to create a memoir together?"

If your EP chooses to continue:
- Agree as to how the method needs to be changed to make it better for your EP.
- Confirm the day/time/place as being appropriate or change as necessary.
- Record for your records: EP name, EP phone number/e-mail, session dates, times, place (consistent preferred):
- Complete the agreement template page.
- Leave your EP with the folder containing the agreement page and help place it where you both can find it again.
- Have your EP write the scheduled session(s) on his/her calendar.
- Provide expectation for the next session.
  - You'll present a draft page of the memoir from this sample session.
  - You'll help your EP sort through his/her memorabilia to choose 3-7 for the memoir.

REMEMBER TO:
- Take photos of memorabilia, pets, other folks, photos, etc. relevant to the sample session.
- Discuss the items to consider for the memoir for the next session. Selecting the items is one of the most important steps. You will do this again in Session 2.
- Offer as appropriate: Optional EP Homework: List 7 or more photos/items for the memoir

FOR THE NEXT SESSION

1. FOLLOW UP: Add narrative and the memoir item photo from your sample session to the template. Print a copy of the page to give your EP at the next session.

2. SESSION 2 TEMPLATE: Print a copy of the template cover page to use with your EP during the next session.

TEMPLATE (SAMPLE) SESSION 1: MP Note-taking Memory#1

MP DIRECTIONS:

Ask baseline questions to add detail and depth to your conversation, for example: 1. Tell me a little about this photo/item. 2. How did you come to have it? (Listen for the who, what, when, where, why, and how.) 3. What was high point of the experience? 4. What obstacle(s) did you have to overcome? 5. How did it end? 6. What did you learn from the experience? 7. What impact did it have on you and your hopes and dreams? 8. Why is it important that this photo/item be in your memoir?

Practice reflective listening by summarizing or paraphrasing your EP's comments, (e.g. "What I hear you saying is ..."). **Use additional prompts by category in Appendix H.** Your EP adds sensory details, character/personality traits, family sayings, anecdotes, favorite books, music, hobbies, interests, songs, lyrics, quotes, poems, letters, diaries, journals, humor.

Notes about the memorabilia/memory #1 Item:_____

Continued notes about the memorabilia/memory #1

TEMPLATE SESSION 1: Agreement to Partner

EP name:

EP phone number:

Memoir partner name:

Memoir partner phone number:

Memoir sessions date/day (consistent preferred):

Memoir sessions time (consistent preferred):

Memoir sessions place (consistent preferred):

Miscellaneous notes:

TEMPLATE SESSION 1: OPTIONAL EP HOMEWORK

<u>LIST 7+ PHOTOS/ITEMS FOR THE MEMOIR</u>

EP DIRECTIONS: List items including photos, scrapbooks, diaries, journals, collections, awards, medals, certificates, letters, e-mail, blogs, speeches, poems, artwork, etc.

1.

2.

3.

4.

5.

6.

7.

TEMPLATE SESSION 1: Draft (Memory 1)

MP DIRECTIONS: 1. Add the narrative from your EP's sample conversation on this page. Be sure to write the memory in first person (I, me, we, us).2. Substitute the photo to the left with the photo of your EP's memorabilia. (Ideally the photo is 200 dpi for printing in the memoir.)

SESSION 2

The Draft Cover Page, Item List, and Message

REMEMBER TO BRING SESSION 2 MATERIALS:

- Completed sample session memory with photo

- Draft Cover Page (blank)

- Item List/Associated Importance (blank)

- Message (blank)

Open the session on a high note.

- Start by giving your EP the finished page from the sample session.

- Choose to have your EP read it or you read it aloud to your EP.

- Note any changes the EP would like to make.

Creating a Draft Cover Page

The draft cover page imparts reality to the memoir and provides a visual image to increase motivation. This draft may change and you will finalize the cover material later. For now, show the TEMPLATE Sample Cover Page.

Ask your EP to:

- Consider the various photos/memorabilia items s/he brought to the table.

- Choose an item for the cover photo.

- Determine a title and dedication.

- Say the title out loud as if introducing it to readers. If it feels like too much, it's too long. It's best to keep the title short and to the point, high concept. A good title captures attention in a second!

Listing 3-7 Selected Items and Importance

This step is vital to the overall depth and impact of the memoir.
Ask your EP:

- Why is this item important to you?

- What influence did it have on your life?

- What message do you want your readers to get from your memoir?

Focusing on the Message

Every story has a theme or a message—what the reader takes away from it. This step is an important introduction to the message the EP wants to convey.

Ask your EP:

- What message do you want your memoir to convey?

- What do you want the reader to remember about you?

Your EP may not have the answer at first. It requires some thought and insight. And it may change later. For now, ask your EP to:

- Repeat the message and revise as necessary.

- Decide if the selected items convey the message.

- Exchange memorabilia items until s/he is satisfied with the items as being in sync with the message.

Write your EP's message on a slip of paper and put it where s/he will see it often—on a desk, or computer, or mirror—wherever your EP can read it frequently.

> *My message is OR*

> *From my memoir, I want readers to remember about me that*

Refer to it as you and your EP write and revise the memoir. You will return to the theme again and again. Change it as new and better ideas come to mind. Remember, keep it to one sentence.

REMEMBER TO:

OFFER AS APPROPRIATE: OPTIONAL TEMPLATE: YOUR MEMOIR COVER (TITLE/PHOTO/DEDICATION)

Even though you have created a draft memoir cover together, your EP can continue to come up with new ideas for the title, photo, and dedication.

FOR THE NEXT SESSION

Print a hard copy of the cover page to show how it may actually look.

Print a hard copy of the list of seven items and the message.

TEMPLATE: Final list of the memories (blank)

TEMPLATE Sequence (blank)

TEMPLATE SESSION 2: Sample Cover Page

MP DIRECTIONS: Do this with your EP in Session 2. Then present the typed draft cover page with photo and dedication in the next session.

Memoir Title

Author Name

Dedication

TEMPLATE SESSION 2: Importance of Items

MP DIRECTIONS: Discuss and complete with your EP.

<u>Memorabilia</u>   <u>Why it's important</u>

1.

2.

3.

4.

5.

6.

7.

Focus on the Message of the 3-7 Items

MP Directions: Every story has a theme or a message—what the reader takes away from it. **Write your EP's message on a slip of paper and put it where s/he will see it often**—on a desk, or computer, or mirror—wherever your EP can read it frequently.

My message is ...

OR

From my memoir, I want readers to remember about me that ...

TEMPLATE SESSION 2: OPTIONAL EP HOMEWORK

MEMOIR COVER(TITLE/PHOTO/DEDICATION)

EP DIRECTIONS: List other title, photo, and dedication ideas on this page.

List memoir title ideas:

1.

2.

3.

4.

5.

List cover photo ideas:

1.

2.

3.

4.

5.

List dedication ideas:

1.

2.

3.

4.

5.

The 3-7 Memorabilia Refined and Sequenced

REMEMBER SESSION 3 MATERIALS:

- Hard copy of the draft cover page

- Hard copy of the list of seven items and the message

- TEMPLATE: Final list of the memories (blank)

- TEMPLATE Sequence (blank)

- TEMPLATE: Summary Sheet Before You Write (blank)

Open the Session on a High Note:

Present the draft cover page from the last session—showing the title, cover photo, and dedication. Put it where your EP will see it often.

Revising the Memorabilia Items

Refine your EP's list. Below are questions related to hopes and dreams and awesome experiences to evoke additional memories. Consider your EP's answers to these questions:

Ask your EP to consider the memorabilia items, do they:

- Reflect your dreams and goals when you were younger?

- Show an awesome (or if preferred, a bad) experience that had a great impact on your life?

- Convey what you are proudest of so far?

- Relate memorable words of advice you received in your lifetime?

- Include values by which your life has taken shape?

- Reflect your strong personality traits? (See Personality Traits in Appendix H)

- Show your weak personality traits? (See Personality Traits in Appendix H)

- Reveal other things the reader should know about you?

Use the TEMPLATE Sequence for Impact

Realize, every story has a beginning, middle, and end. Many memoirs are written in chronological order, as events happened. You are not limited to that sequence. The memories should be sequenced to be dramatic—starting with a pivotal point, then sprinkling in the back story details, including flashbacks. You will want to make sure to include transitions that help the reader understand how everything fits together.

Ask:

- Which of your 3-7 memories makes a good beginning?

- Which memory marks the dramatic highpoint?

- Which memory makes a good ending?

- Where will the remaining memories go?

Start with memorabilia #   the memory about

Next memorabilia#(s)

The high point is memorabilia #   the memory about

Next memorabilia#(s)

End with memorabilia # the memory about

Use the TEMPLATE: Putting it All Together—A Summary Sheet Before You Write

- **Overall Message/Theme:**

- **List the 3-7 memorabilia items in the final sequence.**

- **Memorabilia/Importance**

Offer: OPTIONAL EP TEMPLATE: ADDED IMPORTANCE OF ITEMS

FOR THE NEXT SESSION

Take photos of the chosen memorabilia. Address the cover material again and Identify one photo for the front/inside cover and ponder the title and dedication. This may change as the memoir progresses.

Be sure to save/name the digital photos for easy reference and access, e.g, grandma, postcard, letter, etc.

TEMPLATE SESSION 3 (Option to Skip or Move This Session)

Memorabilia Refined and Sequenced

MP DIRECTIONS: Discuss and complete with your EP.

Refine and finalize the memories:

Memorabilia	Importance
1.	
2.	
3.	
4.	
5.	
6.	
7.	

TEMPLATE SESSION 3: Sequence for Impact

MP DIRECTIONS: Discuss and complete with your EP.

Start with memorabilia #   the memory about

Next memorabilia#(s)

Next memorabilia#(s)

The high point is memorabilia #   the memory about

Next memorabilia#(s)

Next memorabilia#(s)

End with memorabilia # the memory about

TEMPLATE SESSION 3: Summarize Before You Write

MP DIRECTIONS: Discuss and complete with your EP.

Overall Message/Theme:

List the 3-7 memorabilia items in the final sequence.

	Memorabilia	*Why it's important*
1.		
2.		
3.		
4.		
5.		
6.		
7.		

TEMPLATE SESSION 3: OPTIONAL EP HOMEWORK: ADDED IMPORTANCE OF ITEMS

EP DIRECTIONS: List the photos/memorabilia and the added importance of each below. (The awesome or bad experience, significant advice, personality(s) shown, values reflected, other things about you readers should know.)

ITEM	WHY IT'S IMPORTANT
1.	
2.	
3.	
4.	
5.	
6.	
7.	

Basics and Optional Homework Templates

Use the designated template page for EACH of the 3-7 memorabilia items.

Focus on the each item in sequence, first to last. Ask baseline questions to add detail and depth to your conversation, for example:

1. Tell me a little about this photo/item.

2. How did you come to have it? (Listen for the who, what, when, where, why, and how.)

3. What was high point of the experience?

4. What obstacle(s) did you have to overcome?

5. How did it end?

6. What did you learn from the experience?

7. What impact did it have on you and your hopes and dreams?

8. Why is it important that this photo/item be in your memoir?

Practice reflective listening by summarizing or paraphrasing your EP's comments, (e.g. "What I hear you saying is ..."). Use additional prompts by category in Appendix H. Your EP adds sensory details, character/personality traits, family sayings, anecdotes, favorite books, music, hobbies, interests, songs, lyrics, quotes, poems, letters, diaries, journals, humor.

Notes about the memorabilia/memory #____ Item:_____

OPTIONAL EP TEMPLATES: ADD ZEST TO THE MEMORIES

(If appropriate for your EP, copy and use for EACH of the 3-7 memorabilia items.)

Your EP adds sensory details, personality traits, family sayings, anecdotes, favorite books, music, hobbies, interests, songs, lyrics, quotes, poems, etc.

FOR THE NEXT SESSIONS

Start each of the next sessions showing the finished sample page from the previous session. Read it aloud to your EP. Make any changes needed. Add EP's independent work as relevant.

TEMPLATE SESSION 4: (Memory 2) MP Note-taking Pages

MP DIRECTIONS:

Ask baseline questions to add detail and depth to your conversation, for example: 1. Tell me a little about this photo/item. 2. How did you come to have it? (Listen for the who, what, when, where, why, and how.) 3. What was high point of the experience? 4. What obstacle(s) did you have to overcome? 5. How did it end? 6. What did you learn from the experience? 7. What impact did it have on you and your hopes and dreams? 8. Why is it important that this photo/item be in your memoir?

Practice reflective listening by summarizing or paraphrasing your EP's comments, (e.g. "What I hear you saying is ..."). **Use additional prompts by category in Appendix H.** Your EP adds sensory details, character/personality traits, family sayings, anecdotes, favorite books, music, hobbies, interests, songs, lyrics, quotes, poems, letters, diaries, journals, humor.

Notes about the memorabilia/memory #2 Item:_____

Continued notes about the memorabilia/memory #2

TEMPLATE: FINISHED PAGES MEMORY 2

MP DIRECTIONS: Add the narrative from your EP's sample conversation on this page. Be sure to write the memory in first person (I, me, we, us). Substitute the photo to the left with the photo of your EP's memorabilia. (Ideally the photo is 200 dpi for printing in the memoir.)

TEMPLATE SESSION 4: OPTIONAL EP HOMEWORK

ADD ZEST TO YOUR MEMORY

EP DIRECTIONS: Add sensory details, personality traits, family sayings, anecdotes, favorite books, music, hobbies, interests, songs, lyrics, quotes, poems, etc.

Memory #2
Item:_____

TEMPLATE SESSION 5: (Memory 3) MP Note-taking Pages

MP DIRECTIONS:

Ask baseline questions to add detail and depth to your conversation, for example: 1. Tell me a little about this photo/item. 2. How did you come to have it? (Listen for the who, what, when, where, why, and how.) 3. What was high point of the experience? 4. What obstacle(s) did you have to overcome? 5. How did it end? 6. What did you learn from the experience? 7. What impact did it have on you and your hopes and dreams? 8. Why is it important that this photo/item be in your memoir?

Practice reflective listening by summarizing or paraphrasing your EP's comments, (e.g. "What I hear you saying is ..."). **Use additional prompts by category in Appendix H.** Your EP adds sensory details, character/personality traits, family sayings, anecdotes, favorite books, music, hobbies, interests, songs, lyrics, quotes, poems, letters, diaries, journals, humor.

Notes about the memorabilia/memory #3 Item:_____

Continued notes about the memorabilia/memory #3

TEMPLATE: FINISHED PAGES MEMORY 3

MP DIRECTIONS: Add the narrative from your EP's sample conversation on this page. Be sure to write the memory in first person (I, me, we, us). Substitute the photo to the left with the photo of your EP's memorabilia. (Ideally the photo is 200 dpi for printing in the memoir.)

TEMPLATE SESSION 5: OPTIONAL EP HOMEWORK

ADD ZEST TO YOUR MEMORY

EP DIRECTIONS: Add sensory details, personality traits, family sayings, anecdotes, favorite books, music, hobbies, interests, songs, lyrics, quotes, poems, etc.

Memory #3
Item:_____

TEMPLATE SESSION 6: (Memory 4) MP Note-taking Pages

MP DIRECTIONS:

Ask baseline questions to add detail and depth to your conversation, for example: 1. Tell me a little about this photo/item. 2. How did you come to have it? (Listen for the who, what, when, where, why, and how.) 3. What was high point of the experience? 4. What obstacle(s) did you have to overcome? 5. How did it end? 6. What did you learn from the experience? 7. What impact did it have on you and your hopes and dreams? 8. Why is it important that this photo/item be in your memoir?

Practice reflective listening by summarizing or paraphrasing your EP's comments, (e.g. "What I hear you saying is ..."). **Use additional prompts by category in Appendix H.** Your EP adds sensory details, character/personality traits, family sayings, anecdotes, favorite books, music, hobbies, interests, songs, lyrics, quotes, poems, letters, diaries, journals, humor.

Notes about the memorabilia/memory #4 Item:_____

Continued notes about the memorabilia/memory #4

TEMPLATE FINISHED PAGES MEMORY 4

MP DIRECTIONS: Add the narrative from your EP's sample conversation on this page. Be sure to write the memory in first person (I, me, we, us). Substitute the photo to the left with the photo of your EP's memorabilia. (Ideally the photo is 200 dpi for printing in the memoir.)

TEMPLATE SESSION 6: OPTIONAL HOMEWORK

ADD ZEST TO YOUR MEMORY

EP DIRECTIONS: Add sensory details, personality traits, family sayings, anecdotes, favorite books, music, hobbies, interests, songs, lyrics, quotes, poems, etc.

Memory #4

Item:_____

TEMPLATE SESSION 7: (Memory 5) MP Note-taking Pages

MP DIRECTIONS:

Ask baseline questions to add detail and depth to your conversation, for example: 1. Tell me a little about this photo/item. 2. How did you come to have it? (Listen for the who, what, when, where, why, and how.) 3. What was high point of the experience? 4. What obstacle(s) did you have to overcome? 5. How did it end? 6. What did you learn from the experience? 7. What impact did it have on you and your hopes and dreams? 8. Why is it important that this photo/item be in your memoir?

Practice reflective listening by summarizing or paraphrasing your EP's comments, (e.g. "What I hear you saying is …"). **Use additional prompts by category in Appendix H.** Your EP adds sensory details, character/personality traits, family sayings, anecdotes, favorite books, music, hobbies, interests, songs, lyrics, quotes, poems, letters, diaries, journals, humor.

Notes about the memorabilia/memory #5 Item:_____

Continued notes about the memorabilia/memory #5

TEMPLATE FINISHED PAGES MEMORY 5

MP DIRECTIONS: Add the narrative from your EP's sample conversation on this page. Be sure to write the memory in first person (I, me, we, us). Substitute the photo to the left with the photo of your EP's memorabilia. (Ideally the photo is 200 dpi for printing in the memoir.)

TEMPLATE SESSION 7: OPTIONAL EP HOMEWORK

ADD ZEST TO YOUR MEMORY

EP DIRECTIONS: Add sensory details, personality traits, family sayings, anecdotes, favorite books, music, hobbies, interests, songs, lyrics, quotes, poems, etc.

Memory #5

Item:_____

TEMPLATE SESSION 8: (Memory 6) MP Note-taking Pages

MP DIRECTIONS:

Ask baseline questions to add detail and depth to your conversation, for example: 1. Tell me a little about this photo/item. 2. How did you come to have it? (Listen for the who, what, when, where, why, and how.) 3. What was high point of the experience? 4. What obstacle(s) did you have to overcome? 5. How did it end? 6. What did you learn from the experience? 7. What impact did it have on you and your hopes and dreams? 8. Why is it important that this photo/item be in your memoir?

Practice reflective listening by summarizing or paraphrasing your EP's comments, (e.g. "What I hear you saying is ..."). **Use additional prompts by category in Appendix H.** Your EP adds sensory details, character/personality traits, family sayings, anecdotes, favorite books, music, hobbies, interests, songs, lyrics, quotes, poems, letters, diaries, journals, humor.

Notes about the memorabilia/memory #6 Item:_____

Continued notes about the memorabilia/memory #6

TEMPLATE FINISHED PAGES MEMORY 6

MP DIRECTIONS: Add the narrative from your EP's sample conversation on this page. Be sure to write the memory in first person (I, me, we, us). Substitute the photo to the left with the photo of your EP's memorabilia. (Ideally the photo is 200 dpi for printing in the memoir.)

TEMPLATE SESSION 8: OPTIONAL EP HOMEWORK

ADD ZEST TO YOUR MEMORY

EP DIRECTIONS: Add sensory details, personality traits, family sayings, anecdotes, favorite books, music, hobbies, interests, songs, lyrics, quotes, poems, etc.

Memory #6
Item:_____

TEMPLATE SESSION 9: (Memory 7) MP Note-taking Pages

MP DIRECTIONS:

Ask baseline questions to add detail and depth to your conversation, for example: 1. Tell me a little about this photo/item. 2. How did you come to have it? (Listen for the who, what, when, where, why, and how.) 3. What was high point of the experience? 4. What obstacle(s) did you have to overcome? 5. How did it end? 6. What did you learn from the experience? 7. What impact did it have on you and your hopes and dreams? 8. Why is it important that this photo/item be in your memoir?

Practice reflective listening by summarizing or paraphrasing your EP's comments, (e.g. "What I hear you saying is ..."). **Use additional prompts by category in Appendix H.** Your EP adds sensory details, character/personality traits, family sayings, anecdotes, favorite books, music, hobbies, interests, songs, lyrics, quotes, poems, letters, diaries, journals, humor.

Notes about the memorabilia/memory #7 Item:_____

Continued notes about the memorabilia/memory #7

TEMPLATE: FINISHED PAGES MEMORY 7

MP DIRECTIONS: Add the narrative from your EP's sample conversation on this page. Be sure to write the memory in first person (I, me, we, us). Substitute the photo to the left with the photo of your EP's memorabilia. (Ideally the photo is 200 dpi for printing in the memoir.)

TEMPLATE SESSION 9: OPTIONAL EP HOMEWORK

ADD ZEST TO YOUR MEMORY

EP DIRECTIONS: Add sensory details, personality traits, family sayings, anecdotes, favorite books, music, hobbies, interests, songs, lyrics, quotes, poems, etc.

Memory #7

Item:_____

CHECK-UP SESSION

VOILA! The First Draft

FOR THE CHECK-UP SESSION:

Put It All Together

- **Make two copies of all the finished memoir pages to review with your EP. Be sure to include the title page (with photo and dedication).**

    - If you have downloaded the template digital file from 7Memories.com, copy/paste the finished memoir pages into the final template. Note that the session template pages are in Verdana 14pt whereas the final template is in large print format (HevLight 18pt). Your copy/paste will overwrite the Alice Fern template.

    - Or open a blank document file in your computer for copying/pasting this draft of the finished memoir.

- Review the 14-item check-up sheet to eliminate any items that may not be appropriate for your EP.

- Use the 14-Item Check-up as optional EP homework if appropriate.

The 14-Item Check-up

MP DIRECTIONS: Discuss the questions as appropriate for your EP.

1. Does the memoir start with a powerful beginning that whisks your reader from the room and transports him/her into your story?

Hint: Start the story with dramatic flair. Perhaps your EP had a change in his/her normal life—s/he began a journey, a mysterious/important letter arrived or a stranger appeared at his/her door. Perhaps a magical or mystifying event took place. Perhaps s/he found a strange object. Whatever the incident, show how it took your EP from the ordinary routine and launched the story. Or consider a "flashback" approach, starting with the present experience tied to your EP's memoir, then transitioning to the rest of the memoir. In the "flashback" technique, be sure to come full circle, back to the starting point.

___Yes ____No   Notes to yourself:

2. Does it maintain interest in the middle?

Hint: Plant a surprise, a complication or a change of direction. You don't want things to go smoothly. You want some problems to crop up and tension to increase as the memoir progresses. This will reflect your EP's strong personality traits and show his/her determination to achieve his/her life's ambitions.

___Yes ____No   Notes to yourself:

3 Does the ending tie everything together?

Hint: Make sure the ending is clear and the memoir does not just stop. Perhaps it comes full circle from the beginning.

___Yes ____No   Notes to yourself:

4. Do the facts and ideas flow in a logical and sensible manner to move the memoir forward?

Hint: Make sure every sentence pertains to the memory. If a sentence does not "sound right" make sure it is "on message." Then try removing it to see if it is really needed. If not, keep it out of the memoir. Move sentences around to create a better flow.

___Yes ____No   Notes to yourself:

5. Does it include insight and reflection?

Hint: This relates to how the experience influenced your EP and why it's important to him/her. Be sure to add some reflection, looking back on it now. Such thoughts will add great depth to the memoir and will reflect the theme and personality traits discussed earlier.

___Yes ____No   Notes to yourself:

6. Does it SHOW the personality traits your EP wants readers to remember about him/her?

Hint: Telling is when you describe what is happening. (For example: James waited outside the headmaster's door feeling awful.) Showing relates happenings using actions and reactions. (For example: Stomach churning, James stared at the headmaster's door. He knew he'd be dead meat the moment it opened.) SHOWING grabs interest. Words like *churning, stared*, and *dead meat* are strong, active and paint a memorable instant picture in your reader's head.

___Yes ____No   Notes to yourself:

7. Does it include careful description?

Hint: The goal is to include the right amount of description—but not so much that the reader gets lost in the details. The trick is to use description sparingly, including only the most significant and compelling information. It's most effective at its briefest and cleanest, when it sparks images in the reader's mind, but does not provide an exact portrait. (For example, with people, notice personality traits, quirks, gestures, and body movement. Recall conversations, jokes, and quips.)

___Yes ___No   Notes to yourself:

8. Does it use vivid language to create word pictures or mini-movies that ignite the reader's imagination?

Hint: Use specific nouns—castle, giant, dwarf, Cyclops. Use active, exciting verbs, especially those that sound like their meaning such as: thump, whack, bang, whiz, crash, crunch, plop, sizzle, pop, slam, whir, pop, twirl, mince.

___Yes ___No   Notes to yourself:

9. Is there variety in the length of paragraphs and sentences?

Hint: Long sentences help paint pictures. Short sentences provide punch.

___Yes ___No   Notes to yourself

10. Is it the appropriate length?

Hint: The length does not matter. More important is to keep the reader engaged with vivid language and variety.

___Yes ___No   Notes to yourself:

11. Does it include a variety of material to make it interesting to the reader?

Hint: Sprinkle the memoir with some zest: descriptions, quotes, and other items to add interest and show your EP's strong suits. In deciding on what to include, think of the readers. Ask: Will this interest the readers?

___Yes ___No   Notes to yourself:

12. Does the memoir have the appropriate voice?

Hint: Write as if you are telling the story to someone, using active voice. This will result in a natural writing style. Regardless of whether your EP's personal style is humorous or poignant, you want to give the memoir a sense of honesty and vivacity.

___Yes ____No   Notes to yourself:

13. NOW, BACK TO THE THEME: Does your memoir convey the message your EP wants?

Hint: Refer to the theme again. What does your memoir say about your EP? Change the memoir as needed to reflect the theme. (Or revise the theme accordingly.)

___Yes ____No   Notes to yourself:

14. Are you or your EP concerned about the memoir in general? Or about a particular aspect of the memoir?

Hint: Read the problematic area(s) of the memoir again—out of context. Identify exactly what is not right: The idea? The language? Or? Reread the items above to find hints for fixing the problem(s). If it is a sentence or paragraph, move it or leave it out and see if the change makes it better.

___Yes ____No   Notes to yourself

FOR THE NEXT SESSION

- **Make the changes agreed upon by your EP and you.**

- **Use the TEMPLATE to create the final draft. Add the title with the cover photo and dedication, followed by each of the 3-7 memory pages with photos.**

- **Print two copies for use with your EP.**

TEMPLATE CHECK-UP: OPTIONAL EP HOMEWORK

14 ITEM CHECK-UP

MP DIRECTIONS: Print the 14 item check-up for your EP to use independently during the week. Eliminate any items that may not be appropriate for your EP.

14 Questions to Consider

1. Does the memoir start with a powerful beginning that whisks your reader from the room and transports him/her into your story?

Hint: Start the story with dramatic flair. Perhaps your EP had a change in his/her normal life—s/he began a journey, a mysterious/important letter arrived or a stranger appeared at his/her door. Perhaps a magical or mystifying event took place. Perhaps s/he found a strange object. Whatever the incident, show how it took your from the ordinary routine and launched the story. Or consider a "flashback" approach, starting with the present experience tied to your EP's memoir, then transitioning to the rest of the memoir. In the "flashback" technique, be sure to come full circle, back to the starting point.

____Yes ____No   Notes to yourself:

2. Does it maintain interest in the middle?

Hint: Plant a surprise, a complication or a change of direction. You don't want things to go smoothly. You want some problems to crop up and tension to increase as the memoir progresses. This will reflect your EP's strong personality traits and show his/her determination to achieve your life's ambitions.

____Yes ____No   Notes to yourself:

3 Does the ending tie everything together?

Hint: Make sure the ending is clear and the story does not just stop. Perhaps it comes full circle from the beginning.

____Yes ____No   Notes to yourself:

4. Do the facts and ideas flow in a logical and sensible manner to move the story forward?

Hint: Make sure every sentence pertains to the memory. If a sentence does not "sound right" make sure it is "on message." Then try removing it to see if it is really needed. If not, keep it out of the memoir. Move sentences around to create a better flow.

____Yes ____No   Notes to yourself:

5. Does it include insight and reflection?

Hint: This relates to how the experience influenced your EP and why it's important to him/her. Be sure to add some reflection, looking back on it now. Such thoughts will add great depth to the memoir and will reflect the theme and personality traits discussed earlier.

___Yes ____No   Notes to yourself:

6. Does it SHOW the personality traits your EP wants readers to remember about him/her?

Hint: Telling is when you describe what is happening. (For example: James waited outside the headmaster's door feeling awful.) Showing relates happenings using actions and reactions. (For example: Stomach churning, James stared at the headmaster's door. He knew he'd be dead meat the moment it opened.) SHOWING grabs interest. Words like *churning, stared*, and *dead meat* are strong, active and paint a memorable instant picture in your reader's head.

___Yes ____No   Notes to yourself:

7. Does it include careful description?

Hint: The goal is to include the right amount of description— but not so much that the reader gets lost in the details. The trick is to use description sparingly, including only the most significant and compelling information. It's most effective at its briefest and cleanest, when it sparks images in the reader's mind, but does not provide an exact portrait. (For example, with people, notice personality traits, quirks, gestures, and body movement. Recall conversations, jokes, and quips.)

___Yes ___No   Notes to yourself:

8. Does it use vivid language to create word pictures or mini-movies that ignite your reader's imagination?

Hint: Use specific nouns—castle, giant, dwarf, Cyclops. Use active, exciting verbs, especially those that sound like their meaning such as: thump, whack, bang, whiz, crash, crunch, plop, sizzle, pop, slam, whir, pop, twirl, mince.

___Yes ___No   Notes to yourself:

9. Is there variety in the length of paragraphs and sentences**?**

Hint: Long sentences help paint pictures. Short sentences provide punch.

___Yes ___No   Notes to yourself

10. Is it the appropriate length?

Hint: The length does not matter. More important is to keep the reader engaged with vivid language and variety

____Yes ____No   Notes to yourself:

11. Does it include a variety of material to make it interesting to the reader?

Hint: Sprinkle the memoir with some zest: descriptions, quotes, and other items to add interest and show your EP's strong suits. In deciding on what to include, think of the readers. Ask: Will this interest the readers?

____Yes ____No   Notes to yourself:

12. Does the memoir have the appropriate voice?

Hint: Write as if you are telling the story to someone, using active voice. This will result in a natural writing style. Regardless of whether your EP's personal style is humorous or poignant, you want to give the memoir a sense of honesty and vivacity.

____Yes ____No   Notes to yourself:

13. NOW, BACK TO THE THEME: Does your memoir convey the message your EP wants?

Hint: Refer to the theme again. What does your memoir say about your EP? Change the memoir as needed to reflect the theme. (Or revise the theme accordingly.)

___Yes ____No   Notes to yourself:

14. Are you or your EP concerned about the memoir in general? Or about a particular aspect of the memoir?

Hint: Read the problematic area(s) of the memoir again—out of context. Identify exactly what is not right: The idea? The language? Or? Reread the items above to find hints for fixing the problem(s). If it is a sentence or paragraph, move it or leave it out and see if the change makes it better.

___*Yes* ____*No*   *Notes to yourself*

Getting to the Finish Line: The Final Review

Taking a Fresh Look at the Memoir.

1. Provide printed copies of the final draft.
2. Use the methods below to review the memoir with your EP.
3. Make notes of revisions needed in your copy so you can make the changes before printing and distributing the finished memoir.
4. Plan for the last session to be a celebration of your partnering together and showing off the final result, your EP's fantastic memoir.

Read the memoir aloud. Let your EP hear how it sounds. How does it flow? Is it enthralling?

Have your EP close his/her eyes and visualize the memoir as a movie. What actor would play your role? How would s/he act? What would s/he think and say? This will give your EP some distance and objectivity about your memoir.

Read parts of the memoir out of context. Start in the middle or at the end and read the sections aloud out of context. How does the passage sound? Does it flow logically? Make sense? Have enough interesting elements?

Add relevant miscellaneous items to the memoir. Ask your EP to identify other significant items such as mottos, letters, certificates, poems, etc. Incorporate them at the end or within the memoir as appropriate.

Planning for the Last Session

Remind your EP that the next session is the last for creating the memoir. You will present the final print copy and a digital file so your EP can make more copies and distribute.

Discuss the numerous print/distribution options once the memoir is in PDF format

- Convert the original document file to PDF format to distribute the memoir. If it's too big for e-mail, upload it to the cloud (Google drive, Dropbox), and e-mail the link so your EP's friends and family can download it.

- Consider upgrading the look of the memoir by copy/pasting it into a professional template. See http://www.bookdesigntemplates.com/template-gallery/.

- Make copies on your home printer or use an online commercial service such as Mixbooks.com or Shutterfly.com or take it to a FedEx/Kinko's or other local printing service for hard copies.

- Save and distribute on a compact disk (CD), memory stick, via e-mail, or through a social media network.

- Convert to an online paperback or e-book format using Createspace.com (24-page minimum) or Kindle Direct Publishing.

- Supplement the printed version with an audio recording of your EP reading his/her memoir.

- Go all out with an audio-visual version, a slide show of the photos accompanied by voice over of your EP reading his/her memoir. Include some favorite music too!

Ask your EP if there's anything special s/he would like to do during the last session. Would other folks be invited to share in the excitement and celebrate the finished memoir? Whatever your EP decides, plan to make it happen.

TEMPLATE NEXT-TO-LAST SESSION: OPTIONAL EP HOMEWORK

FRIENDS/FAMILY DISTRIBUTION LIST

EP Directions: List folks who will get your memoir.

NAME   **E-mail or Snail Mail**

1.

2.

3.

4.

5.

6.

7.

FOR THE NEXT SESSION

1. Make the necessary changes to the final draft.

2. Proofread the memoir at least twice. (See Appendix F for Proven Proofreading Techniques.)

3. **Print a copy for your EP and provide a digital file on a thumb drive, CD, or on cloud storage.**

LAST SESSION

The Finished Memoir

Reading Together

Ask your EP how s/he would like to read the final memoir—silently, or aloud with one of you reading to the other.

Take the time to savor the photos and writing on each page.

Help your EP with listing the friends and family who will get the memoir.

Celebrating Your Shared Accomplishment!

Honor your EP's wishes to celebrate you discussed together in the previous session.

Invite family members, friends, caretakers, etc. as appropriate.

Take a photo of your celebration to post to your EP's family and friends.

Engage in a Skype or video chat with distant family members and friends.

Getting Final EP Feedback

What did your EP especially like about the Memoir Partnering Method?

What did s/he especially not like about it? How would s/he change it?

Did the method have any impact on your EP? If so, describe.

Would your EP recommend that others do this? Why or why not?

APPENDICES A-K

APPENDIX A

Frequently Asked Questions About the Standard Memoir Partnering Method

Why should I help my EP write a memoir?

Your EP has experiences and wisdom to pass on to family, friends, and future generations. And there may not be much time left to help him/her evoke these memories. Your kind generosity of time will create an invaluable bond and show your EP that his/her life is worthwhile and important to others. (See the *Benefits* section for more information.)

What are my responsibilities in creating the memoir?

You are responsible for meeting with your EP on a consistent basis, helping to evoke memories, take notes, and provide finished pages of each memory. (See the *Overview* section for complete details.)

How do I get the digital file of templates?

E-mail: Info@7Memories.com.

What if I hate to type?

Use one of the speech-to-text software programs readily available. Most computers, tablets, and cell phones have them installed as standard software. There are numerous free versions of commercial programs, such as Dragon and Speechnotes. Text-to-speech software has come a long way and can be remarkably accurate.

How many memories should I include?

Tackling seven memories seems to be an appropriate slice of life. For some EPs, three memories may be the most you can write together. Or, your EP may get motivated to do more than seven memories. The method is flexible so tailor it to your EP's level and your time. See the Mini-Memoir (Appendix B) and the Memoir Moments approach (Appendix C) to adapt to memory loss or dementia.

How long are the sessions?

Each session generally takes 30-60 minutes—enough time to review the previous session and move on to the next memory. Again, it's flexible based on your EP and you.

What if my EP is reluctant to create a memoir or does not feel it is necessary?

Use the built-in motivational activities: early on, create the cover title, photo, and dedication to motivate your EP. Respond to any doubts with affirmations. Have those to whom the memoir is dedicated write letters of encouragement. These letters can be included in the memoir. (See *Motivational Activities* section.) Or engage your EP in a mini-memoir that takes only 3 sessions.

What if my EP doesn't identify a photo or memento?

Be observant, like a detective. Look around the room and focus on a photo, collection, or any item on display. Your EP may be wearing something like a ring or pin that can spark a memory. Or ask someone close to your EP to help identify appropriate photos and memorabilia. Or capture stories your EP repeats in casual conversation. Get the details with the *who, what, when, where, how, and why* questions and add others from the prompts in Appendix H.

What if my EP goes off topic?

Be respectful and listen for a while. Bring your EP back to topic by asking about a detail s/he has already given. Then move on to a new prompt.

What if my EP says too much or too little?

For your talkative EP, you'll take lots of notes, then delete irrelevant or repetitive details so the narrative flows well. For your quiet EP, you'll need to ask more questions and probe a bit more. Consider doing some research on the web to add photos and details that will give depth to the memory. Be sure to check with your EP for accuracy ad relevancy of details you discovered.

What if my EP has trouble remembering. Should I enlist the help of their spouse or other person with knowledge of the EP's past?

Use the specific prompts in Appendix F to evoke details. If that doesn't work, try another photo or memento that evokes more memories. Use the Mini-Memoir (Appendix B) or the Memoir Moments approach (Appendix C). Engage others to help as appropriate to your situation. If all else fails, then the Memoir Partnering Method may not be the right fit for your EP and the time has past for creating a memoir together.

How do I partner with an EP who is not local?

There are a number of ways to partner with a non-local EP, such as using digital programs such as Skype/Facetime or engaging in phone sessions. (See the *Adapting for Long Distant EPs* section.}

What if I want to do a memoir of a couple, for example, my grandparents, or siblings?

The method is perfect for creating a couple's version. Simply, have the couple work together to select memorabilia items and provide details. Alternatively, if they have difficulty working together, let them take turns in choosing and discussing items for their memoir. It's always interesting to hear their different points of views while discussing the same item! It works well with siblings too.

Does the Memoir Partnering Method adapt to groups?

Yes. In a small group each group member takes a turn at being the focus for the session, while the others listen. (See the *Adapting the Method to Groups and Families* section.)

How can I engage other family members in the Memoir Partnering Method?

The Memoir Partnering Method is a perfect family activity whereby each member takes a turn creating a memoir page with the EP. Identify one family member to take the lead in scheduling the sessions, collecting the pages, and putting together the final version. Then celebrate together as you present the finished memoir. Imagine how much love your EP feels given this caring attention.

How do I get the memoir printed as a final book?

Paper: Convert the final memoir document to a PDF and print it yourself or send to a local service such as Staples or FedEx-Kinko's. For a more professional looking book, consider online services such as Mixbooks.com or Createspace.com. Be sure the memoir meets any page requirements. Email: Info@7memories.com and check out 7Memories.com for more information.

Digital: Distribute the PDF file by e-mail if the file is not too large. Or use cloud storage, such as Google Drive or DropBox, and provide a link to the document so others can download and read it.

Where can I get help and see other 7 Memories products and services?

The Memoir Partnering Method is a product of **7Memories.com.** Check out the website where you can find help with each stage of your project. Editing and other services are available. Do it yourself: *7 Memories: Write Your Memoir in 28 Days.* And try *MemoirMagic^TM*. E-mail: Info@7Memories.com.

APPENDIX B

The Mini-Memoir for Early-Stage Dementia

	7 MEMORIES (Standard)	MINI-MEMOIR	MEMOIR MOMENTS (Appendix C)
Use of Photos, Memorabilia, and Activities to Spark Memory	✓	✓	✓
Reminiscence Therapy	✓	✓	✓
Reflective Listening	✓	✓	✓
Provides Prompts to Engage in Conversation	200+ Prompts in 18 categories	20 Prompts and Others as Appropriate	Numerous General Prompts
Flexible Number and Length of Sessions	12 +/-	6 +/-	1 +
Creates Custom Reading and Memory Materials	Memoir Book of Any Length	Shorter Memoir Book	Memoir Pages or Flashcards
Examples	✓	✓	✓
Templates	✓		
Optional Homework	✓	✓	✓
Optional Use of Technology	✓	✓	✓

Memoir Partnering in 6+/- Sessions

SESSION	FOCUS	TO-DO	OPTIONAL EP HOMEWORK
SESSION 1 Prompts 1-3	Name, Age, DOB, Close Living Loved Ones	-Explain the Partnering Method -Introduce self: Name, age, DOB, close loved ones -Use Prompts 1-3 -Take a photo/selfie with you and your EP	-List photos, anecdotes, or memories to include in up-coming sessions. -Read narrative from Session 1.
SESSION 2 Prompts 4-7	Education, Career, Interests	-Review Session 1 narrative -Continue with next prompts	-Read/review Session 1. -List photos, anecdotes, or memories to include in up-coming sessions.
SESSION 3 Prompts 8-12	Achievements, Anecdotes, Philosophy	-Review Session 2 narrative -Continue with next prompts	-Read/review Session 2. -List photos, anecdotes, or memories to include in up-coming sessions.
SESSION 4 Cover Page Creation*	Title, Photo, Dedication for cover	-Review Session 3 narrative -Create cover page	-Read/review Session 3. -List photos, anecdotes, or memories to include.
SESSION 5 (Next to Last Session)	Final draft memoir	-Review final draft -Use the 7-Item Check Up	Read/Review final draft.
SESSION 6	Final Memoir	Read together, Distribute, Celebrate	Distribute memoir to family and friends.

*Create a memoir cover in any session as appropriate to motivate your EP.

MP General Directions:

- **Review the Overview material. Be sure to schedule regular Mini-Memoir sessions.**

- Session 1: Start with prompts 1-3 below for the first session. Introduce yourself and the process by sharing your answers to the first three prompts. This builds interest and trust. Remember to: 1) Dig deep with the who, what, where, when, how and why questions for a rich narrative and story. 2) Have a conversation about your EP's responses rather than just ask questions. 3) Take notes to create a narrative in written form using first person, i.e. I, me, we, ours my, mine. 4) Take photos of your EPs associated mementos and photos to copy/paste into the Mini-Memoir. 5) Take a photo of you and your EP to leave the basic narrative of the introductory material. Here's a sample:

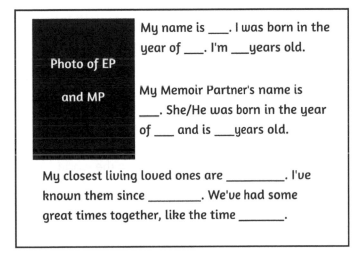

My name is ___. I was born in the year of ___. I'm ___years old.

My Memoir Partner's name is ___. She/He was born in the year of ___ and is ___years old.

Photo of EP and MP

My closest living loved ones are _____. I've known them since _____. We've had some great times together, like the time _____.

- **Sessions 2-3: Bring two copies of the complete narrative from Session 1. Remember to:** 1) Have your EP read the narrative aloud to discuss it or you read it aloud to your EP. 2) Make any changes on your copy for the final draft. 3) Leave one copy of the narrative for your EP to read and review. 4) Continue with questions 4-7 in Session 2, then questions 8-12 in Session 3. As appropriate, add 8 additional questions (next page) or memoir prompts in Appendix H.

- **Session 4: Create a cover page with a photo and dedication.** (See the Alice Fern cover Appendix J.)

- **Session 5: Show the draft memoir.** Review the information with your EP and together use the 7-Item Checkup to make enhancements. Make a list of family and friends to receive the memoir.

- **Session 6: Share the finished memoir with your EP in the last session.** Provide copies of the final mini-memoir for your EP and his/her family and friends.

12 Prompts: Basic Questions (See 8 optional prompts below.)

1. What is your name? Do you have a nickname? How did you get your name/nickname?

2. What is your age? Date and place of birth?

3. Who are your closest living loved ones?

4. What is your highest level of education? What school did you attend?

5. What is/was your profession?

6. Tell me about any service in the military.

7. Do you belong to any fraternal, religious, or civic organizations? What are your interests, hobbies, or volunteer activities?

8. What are you proudest achievements and why?

9. What are your favorite anecdotes and recollections about you?

10. Tell me about an individual or event that had a significant impact on your life.

11. What is your philosophy of life? If you could change the world, what would you do?

12. How you want to be remembered?

Eight Optional Prompts

1. What do you feel most grateful for?

2. What are the most important lessons you've learned in life?

3. What words of wisdom would you like to pass along?

4. What is your happiest memory?

5. How has your life been different than what you'd imagined?

6. Do you have any regrets?

7. What or who is your source of inspiration?

8. If you were to die suddenly this evening, what would you most regret having not told someone?

The 7-Item Check-up
MP Directions: Consider the following with your EP in Session 5

1. Do the facts and ideas flow in a logical and sensible manner to move the memoir forward?

Hint: If a sentence does not "sound right" make sure it is "on message." Then try removing it to see if it is really needed. If not, keep it out of the mini-memoir. Move sentences around to create a better flow.

2. Does it include insight and reflection?

Hint: This relates the influence of the experience and why it's important. Be sure to add some reflection, looking back on it now. Such thoughts will add great depth to the mini-memoir.

3. Does it SHOW personality traits?

Hint: Telling is when you describe what is happening. (For example: James waited outside the headmaster's door feeling awful.) Showing relates happenings using actions and reactions. (For example: Stomach churning, James stared at the headmaster's door. He knew he'd be dead meat the moment it opened.) SHOWING grabs interest. Words like *churning, stared*, and *dead meat* are strong, active and paint a memorable instant picture in your reader's head.

4. Is there variety in the length of paragraphs and sentences?

Hint: The length does not matter. More important is to keep the reader engaged with vivid language and variety. Long sentences help paint pictures. Short sentences provide punch.

5. Does it include a variety of material to make it interesting ?

Hint: Sprinkle the Mini-Memoir with some zest: descriptions, quotes, and other items to add interest and show your EP's strong suits. In deciding on what to include, think of the readers. Ask: Will this interest readers?

6. Does the Mini-Memoir convey the desired message?

Hint: Refer to the theme again. What does the Mini-Memoir say about your EP? Change the Mini-Memoir as needed to reflect the theme. (Or revise the theme accordingly.)

7. Are there any concern about the Mini-Memoir in general? Or about a particular aspect of the Mini-Memoir?

Hint: Read the problematic area(s) of the Mini-Memoir again—out of context. Identify exactly what is not right: The idea? The language? Or? Reread the items above to find hints for fixing the problem(s). If it is a sentence or paragraph, move it or leave it out and see if the change makes it better. Include your EP in this process to the extent possible.

APPENDIX C

Memoir Moments for Middle-Stage Dementia

	7 MEMORIES (Standard)	MINI-MEMOIR (Appendix B)	MEMOIR MOMENTS
Use of Photos, Memorabilia, and Activities to Spark Memory	✓	✓	✓
Reminiscence Therapy	✓	✓	✓
Reflective Listening	✓	✓	✓
Provides Prompts to Engage in Conversation	200+ Prompts in 18 categories	20 Prompts and Others as Appropriate	Numerous General Prompts
Flexible Number and Length of Sessions	12 +/-	6 +/-	1 +
Creates Custom Reading and Memory Materials	Memoir Book of Any Length	Shorter Memoir Book	Memoir Pages or Flashcards
Examples	✓	✓	✓
Templates	✓		
Optional Homework	✓	✓	✓
Optional Use of Technology	✓	✓	✓

Memoir Partnering in 1+ Sessions*

A memoir moment is a snapshot--a moment that makes up our personal stories and reveals who we are as human beings.

FROM THE PAST: It may be a snapshot of a newborn. Or the moment the bride and groom kiss. Or a retirement celebration. Yes, those are momentous events that change our lives and are likely remembered even when recall is fading. As the MP, you use these photos to evoke EP memories.

HAPPENING NOW: Then there are those small moments of humor, heartbreak, or just plain fun that make up our daily lives. **We use the current moments too.**

Introduction with Your EP: What's in a Name?

What's the one thing that everyone has? A name! So exploring your EP's name is a great way to engage in a conversation and get to know him/her. This works well if you are meeting your EP for the first time. And even if you have known your EP for a long time, you are sure to find out something new and interesting.

SESSION OVERVIEW	FOCUS	TO-DO	OPTIONAL EP HOMEWORK
SESSION 1 *	Name, Age, DOB, story about name	-Introduce self: Name, age, DOB -Use prompts 1-7 to discuss name -Take a photo/selfie with you and your EP -Leave session narrative for EP	Read narrative from Session 1.

*Continue with individual Memoir Moment sessions as appropriate for your EP. with the activities in this appendix. Use your imagination and knowledge of your EP to add more activities to the Memoir Moments pages (notecards or flashcards). Create a cover as shown in Appendix B.

MP Directions: Start by introducing the session something like this: "I thought we could start our conversation today talking about names. My first name is_____ but I have a nickname/prefer to be called _____. I'm _____ years old and was born the year of_____ in (place) _____.

Use the prompts below to start a discussion, omitting any prompts that are not appropriate.

1. What about you? Your first name is _____. (Let EP respond here.) Do you have a nickname or a preferred name? _____

2. What is your age?_____ What year were you born?_____ Where?_____

3. Who gave you your name? Tell me a little bit about that person.

4. Were you named for a relative or a famous or favorite person? If so, who? Tell me a little bit about that relative or famous/favorite person.

5. What were some changes to your name and how did they come about, i.e., business, professional, personal, marriage, etc.?

6. If you could change your name, what would you change it to?

7. What names did you give your children? Your pets? Why

Sample Narrative Page to Leave with Your EP

Photo of EP and MP	My name is ___. I was born in the year of ___. I'm ___years old. My Memoir Partner's name is ___. She/He was born in the year of ___ and is ___years old.

My name was given to me by _____ because _____. I like the name ____, my nickname, and I got it when _____.

Six "Name" Activities to Develop with Your EP

From this simple introduction about names, you can create many stimulating activities tailored to your EP. For example:

1. Start a book with the narrative and related photos.

2. Make a family tree or a timeline with your EP showing loved ones' names.

3. Discuss the historical influence when the name was given (politics, movies, music, art, etc.).

4. Have your EP relate a funny and/or memorable story regarding his or her name.

5. Discuss the meaning of the name and how it is like your EP and different from your EP.

6. Discuss the numerology of the name and how the destiny is like your EP and different from your EP.

Six Other Ways to Create Narrative with Your EP

1. Create a Book or flash cards Based on Photos or Memorabilia: Choose from these prompts:

- What can you tell me about this photo/item? Do you remember when it was taken/obtained?

- How did you come to have it? (Listen for the who, what, when, where, why, and how.)

- How did it make you feel (happy/sad/proud)?

- Was there anything hard about it?

- What would you tell others about it?

- Did this change your life in any way? (How?)

- Is this photo/item important to you? (Why?)

On the next page is an excerpt from a Memoir Moments book showing simple recall of name, age, birthplace, and birthdate. **Note that sentences are short, approximately 7-10 words. The book was printed in large type, 18 pt.** The photos add interest and spark memory for the words.

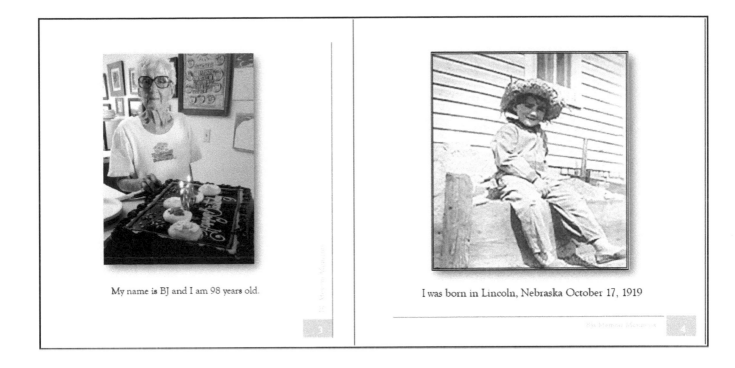

My name is BJ and I am 98 years old.

I was born in Lincoln, Nebraska October 17, 1919

Remember: Consider Font Size

2. Use Current Activities : Consider these prompts:

1.   What is your favorite music/art/food/activity?

2.   When did you first hear/see/taste/ do it?

3.   How did you come to first hear/see/taste/do it? (Listen for the who, what, when, where, why, and how.)

4.   How does it make you feel (happy/sad/proud)?

5.   What would you tell others about it?

6.   Does this change your life in any way? (How?)

7.   Is this music/art/food/activity important to you? (Why?)

3. Evoke a Holiday Memory: Ask about a favorite:

- Photo or memento of that holiday
- Holiday song
- Holiday food
- Holiday smell
- Game, sport, or special tradition (clothing or parade)
- Memory of that holiday

Capture the holiday in photos or video: Have relatives and friends write or say something to your EP about past or present holidays or about gratitude for the EP.

4. Use Today's Technology to Capture Activities:

- Capture an activity with your tablet or cell phone:

- Take a photo of the activity

- Use speech to text software to record what is said and create text

- Copy/paste photo and text onto a page.

- Use prompts to create text:

    1. How did you come to have your first haircut?

    2. Why is getting a haircut important to you?

    3. What would you tell others about it?

feel great when Daniella cuts my hair.

5. For EPs Who are Less Communicative: Use simple YES/NO prompts, then two choices:

- Do you remember the first time you celebrated the holiday? Do you remember how old you were? Or who was with you?
- Do you remember what you did to celebrate that holiday? Did you have any family traditions?
- Do you have a favorite song or music of that holiday?
- Do you remember any smells associated with the holiday? Do you have any favorite foods?
- Did you play any special games or sports or have special traditions or wear special clothing?
- Do you have a favorite memory of that holiday?

NOTE: These prompts require only yes/no at first with the goal of having your EP fill in more details.

Provide two options for your EP: apple/pumpkin pie; white/dark meat; turkey/ham; jazz/classical; baseball/football; tennis/golf

ALSO IMPORTANT: Use Letters from Loved Ones to Stimulate Communication

Below is a letter of gratitude from a grandson. Note the letter is 100 words or less and printed in 18 point font.

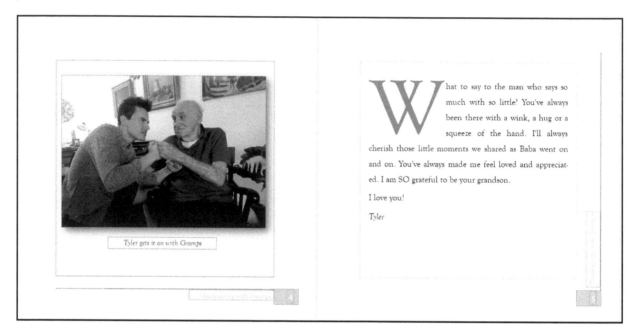

6. Use Photos of Your EP with Loved Ones to Reinforce Facial Recognition and Naming

My three siblings: Rosie, Katie, Me, and Izzie

WORTH REPEATING: Read aloud to your EP and/or use text-to-speech technology to have your EP listen to narrative.

Add Variety and Tailor Sessions Based on Your EP's Interests

Find out about your EP's past interests and hobbies and use simplified versions in subsequent sessions. For example:

- Use simple games and apps on your computer or tablet: math; language; memory, agility, trivia.

- Play paper/pencil games—hangman, anagrams, simple crossword puzzles, other word games.

- Start jigsaw puzzles.

- Play board games like Rumikub, bingo, dominoes, etc.

- Play card games.

- Read aloud: newspaper; fiction; nonfiction; comics; your EP's memoir material

- Create a music playlist—discuss when/where EP listened to music; dance; clap; sing along; print lyrics to sing along

- Integrate activities done in the home, day care programs, or care facility.

- Consider favorites to discuss—foods, hobbies, pets, etc.

- Play games and activities to do with the grandchildren.

Reflective Listening: The First Step in Note-Taking

Reflective listening is a way of responding to your EP that shows you're really listening and that you care. It's a summary or paraphrase of your EP's comments, starting with a phrase such as:

- "So what I hear you saying is …"

- "It sounds like …"

- "It seems as if…."

Your EP will affirm or negate your paraphrase, helping to ensure accuracy. Such paraphrasing leads to efficient notes on each memory—notes that can be enhanced later for inclusion in the memoir. Plus the paraphrase provides an opening to questions leading to deeper memories:

- "That sounds like a challenging time. What do you think made it so interesting/tough/demanding/[insert the appropriate word]?"

- "I'd like to ask you more about [insert the topic.] Do you mind talking about it?"

- "Do you mind if we talk about why you chose this /memorabilia/[insert specific topic]?"

- "It seems you're feeling [insert a reflection] about /[writing your memoir together/insert specific topic]; yes? Why would that be?"

- "Can you tell me how that situation [insert specific topic] is different from today?"

- "You mentioned [insert specific topic]. What was that like for you?"

Reflective listening also presents an opportunity for affirmations. Affirmations are statements used to acknowledge the EP's strengths and successes as s/he delves into the past. Use affirmations to help motivate your EP and to increase confidence in writing the memoir. To make your affirmations sound genuine, tie them to specific memories and memorabilia.

- "Sounds like you were a great father/husband/ grandfather/boss, employee/athlete/[insert the appropriate word] because you were strong/caring/knowledgeable/talented/skilled/[insert the appropriate word]."

- "You really showed a great deal of strength/courage/determination/[insert the EP's behavior] in that situation."

- "With that challenge of [insert specific detail], it's [fantastic/impressive] that you've been so successful in overcoming it."

- "I think a lot of people probably would have felt the same way you did in that situation [insert specific situation]."

APPENDIX E

Writing Tips for Memoir Partners

1. Write your EP's memoir in first person as s/he relates the memory. (I, me, we, us)

2. Use active voice to create a natural writing style.

3. Include powerful descriptions that show your EP's personality traits.

4. Use vivid language to create word pictures that ignite the reader's imagination.

5. Use long sentences to paint pictures and short sentences to add punch.

6. Vary the length of paragraphs and sentences.

7. Include a variety of material to increase interest.

8. Start the memoir with a powerful beginning that transports readers into your EP's world.

9. Maintain interest throughout. Don't let the middle sag.

10. Check that the narrative flows in a logical and sensible manner to move the memoir forward.

11. Tie everything together in the end using the theme and powerful message given by your EP.

12. For long narratives, edit to remove irrelevant or repeated details.

13. For short narratives, ask more questions and research material to add information. Be sure to check with your EP to ensure veracity of the added information.

Proven Proofreading Techniques

Set the memoir aside, at least overnight, before you begin proofreading. You will have a fresher eye if you allow time between the writing and proofreading.

Proofread when you are rested. Set aside one hour when your eyes and mind are rested and you have no distractions.

Have references handy: At a minimum, use a good dictionary and thesaurus. Online references,like the Merriam-Webster, offer both the dictionary and thesaurus free of charge. (http://www.merriam-webster.com/dictionary/) Realize dictionaries offer contradictory spellings and hyphenation information.

Make a first pass with your spell-checker. Use the spell-checker on your computer CAREFULLY. Decide which changes suggested by the computer are accurate. Computer spell-checkers are notoriously bad and make errors. If you are in doubt of the spelling, double check it with your own dictionary.

Try a free version of grammar check. (http://www.grammarly.com/) Grammarly offers some help, but often is wrong in its suggestions. Use this reference tool with caution.

Print a hard copy of the memoir. The printed memoir looks different on paper than on the computer screen. This will give you another perspective on it.

Use a ruler. Place a ruler under the line of print to slow your pace and direct your eyes to a small amount of text at a time

Proofread out of context. Start at the end of the memoir and work up your to the beginning, line by line.

Concentrate on the visual look of the words and sentences. Look at the surface elements without attaching meaning to the words.

Proofread for one type of error at a time. Start with the type of error you make most, spelling, punctuation, or grammar. Repeat the method for other frequent problems in your writing.

Polish the memoir. Break up long sentences. Eliminate repeated words or ideas. Fix awkward spots. Delete unnecessary words, especially too many adjectives and adverbs. Rewrite passive sentences as active.

Next, read the memoir aloud slowly. Listen for differences between what you actually wrote and what you thought you wrote. A variation: Digitally record the memoir as you read it aloud. Then follow along on the hard copy to identify errors.

Ask someone else to proofread the memoir. They can identify sentences that aren't clear, places where you are too wordy, and other issues.

Consider having the memoir professionally edited or proofed. Have another set of eyes proofread your memoir to eliminate spelling, grammar, syntax, and semantic errors—and those nasty typos.

APPENDIX G

Avoiding Writer's Block

If You or Your EP Gets Stuck: 12 Ways to Avoid Writer's Block

1. **Get out your memorabilia.** Look through the photos, scrapbooks, journals, letters, awards, certificates, collections, etc. to revive energy and inspiration.

2. **Listen to your favorite music.** Music can evoke powerful memories and help relive events. Put on some music, sit back with eyes closed, take a deep breath, and relax into the music from the past.

3. **Give it a rest!** Put away the memoir for a day or two. Then return with a fresh look at the memoir and how to revise it.

4. **Be flexible.** Be willing to throw out ideas or sections of text that are causing problems or just don't work.

5. **Plunge Into the Scary Parts.** What's the problem? Poor spelling? Weak transitions? Go ahead and deliberately spell every word incorrectly, write without transitions, don't use any punctuation—do everything you're not supposed to do, and have fun doing it! Draw caricatures of your writing demons, put the dreaded failure behind and move on.

6. **Loosen Your Standards.** There's really no reason to worry about critics or evaluators. Don't correct anything; write in slang; work for 15 minutes; leave notes, like ADD DETAILS HERE or FIX THIS LATER, throughout the memoir—anything that makes it easier to for your EP to remember and you to write.

7. **Continue with whatever part is easiest or most exciting.** Don't let one part of the memoir stump for long. If it's a problem, just skip it and move on to an easier, more appealing part. Continue writing and revising at whatever point seems right to you and your EP. If necessary, begin in the middle, fine. Leave the first sections until later. The reader will never know that you wrote the memoir backward.

8. Use the prompts from Appendix H. Look over the answers to questions to help spark additional ideas and details.

9. Research other material. Have your EP review his/her diary, e-mail, important blogs, text messages, etc. and jot down ideas that come to his/her mind. Add new ideas, re-sequence ideas, and eliminate sentences.

10. Follow a routine. Follow the agreed-upon routine to get into the mood. Wear comfortable clothing, or listen to a particular type of music.

11. Take a break. Physically move around with your EP, stretch, or walk. Get a snack or drink, or just relax for five minutes before starting to work on the memoir again.

12. Stop when you are on a roll. When writing becomes a struggle, try sticking with it and quit at a high point, so that next time you and your EP will be eager to return to the work. Waves of inspiration will come and go. The trick is scheduling the work together to take full advantage of the tides.

Memoir Prompts by Category

Choose the prompts that relate to your EP's message and personality traits, and/or reveal something unusual, different, impressive, memorable, or special about your EP.

Growing Up—Relationships With Family and Friends

1. Where were you born? (town, state, country)

2. Where did you grow up?

1. Describe the first home you remember, the landscape, your neighborhood or the rural area where you grew up.

2. What was it like?

3. How many people lived in your childhood hometown or city?

4. How was your home different from today's homes?

5. What is your earliest memory?

6. What were your parents like? Describe your natural parents, stepparents, adoptive parents or foster parents.

7. How was your relationship with your parents?

8. How did your parents feel about your being a girl/boy?

9. Did you get into trouble? What was the worst thing you did?

10. How many sisters or brothers did you have? Were they older or younger than you? How did you get along with each other? What were they like growing up?

11. Were boys and girls treated differently in your family? How?

12. What did you look like?

13. How would you describe yourself as a child? Were you happy?

14. What is your best memory of childhood? Worst?

15. How would you describe a perfect day when you were young?

16. Did you have a nickname? How did you get it?

17. Who were your best friends? What were they like?

18. When did you first realize that boys and girls were different?

19. Describe your relationship with your peers during your teenage years. How did you feel about yourself during this time? How were you treated by others your age? By adults?

20. Who influenced you as a child? Parents? Grandparents or other relatives? Teacher? Religious figure? A neighbor?

21. When did you first begin to develop romantic attachments to others?

22. What did you think your life would be like when you were older?

23. What kind of life partner did you envision? How did you envision yourself as a partner?

24. Do you recall any special incidents that had a significant impact on you as a child? (an accident, hospitalization, birth of a younger sibling, moving, best friend moving away, divorce, death, family violence, a school project, etc.)

Schooling

1. What kind of schools did you attend? Number of students? What subjects did you like best/least?

2. Did you enjoy school?

3. What kind of student were you?

4. How far did you go in school? Did you complete a degree?

5. What did you do for fun?

6. How would your classmates remember you?

7. Are you still friends with anyone from that time in your life?

8. What are your best and worst memories of high school?

9. Did you continue your education after high school? Why? Where?

10. Did you have any difficulties pursuing further education? (family support, money, etc.)

11. Describe jobs you had as a young person at home. Describe any paid jobs you had outside the home.

12. Did you obtain full-time employment immediately after high school? Why? Describe your jobs. What did you earn?

13. Did you enjoy working? Why or why not?

14. How was your education different from the way children are educated today?

Early Activities (Sports, Hobbies, Interests)

1. What were your typical and favorite childhood activities?

2. Were there any pets, toys, imaginary playmates, books, dolls or games that were especially important to you as a child? Describe them. What influence did they have on your development?

3. Did you belong to any youth groups? Which ones? What influence do you think they played in your development? (for example, Girl Scouts, Camp Fire, 4-H, church or temple youth group)

4. Were you athletic as a child? What sports did you play? Was this acceptable to your family?

5. Have your physical activities and your beliefs about physical activity changed over time?

6. Have you had to limit or focus on your physical activity? If so, how did you react?

7. Are there articles of clothing you once wore you no longer wear?

8. How were these activities different from the way they are done today?

9. What activities in your youth did you enjoy most (playing games/sports, reading, artistic endeavors, community service, etc.)?

First Love

1. When did you first fall in love?

2. Describe your first kiss.

3. How did you lose your virginity? Was it as you thought it would be?

4. What was your first serious relationship?

5. Do you believe in love at first sight?

6. Do you ever think about previous lovers? Who are they? What happened between you two? Have you stayed in touch?

Personality Traits

Identify two strong and two weak personality traits that were influential and reflected in life experiences and events. These will add flavor and depth to the memoir. Add other personality traits as relevant. Match these to experiences that reflect them.

Influential	Moral	Caring	Curious
Courageous	Introspective	Passionate	Assertive
Insightful	Logical	Punctual	Resourceful
Generous	Optimistic	Creative	Bright
Organized	Open-minded	Bold	Expressive
Analytical	Accomplished	Inventive	Risk-taker
Ethical	Receptive	Determined	Industrious
Affectionate	Aspiring	Candid	Quirky
Cheerful	Considerate	Cooperative	Courteous
Decisive	Determined	Devoted	Flexible
Persevering	Enthusiastic	Trusting	Forgiving
Focused	Frugal	Generous	Grateful
Hard-working	Honest	Humble	Involved
Jealous	Kind	Practical	Positive
Punctual	Realistic	Reliable	Respectful
Responsible	Self-confident	Serious	Sincere
Sympathetic	Unselfish	Unpretentious	Work-oriented

Military Experience

1. What year did you enter the military?

2. Why did you serve in the military?

3. In which branch of the military did you serve?

4. What did you do in the military?

5. What is your strongest memory of the military?

6. What was a positive outcome of your service?

7. Who was a memorable character while in the military?

8. How did serving in the military change you?

Adulthood (Long-Term Relationships and Marriage)

1. How did you meet your significant other or husband/wife?

2. How did you know s/he was *the one*?

3. How did you propose or decide to live together?

4. What problems did you encounter in the early years of co-habitation/marriage?

5. Did you ever think of leaving or getting divorced?

6. Did you ever leave or get divorced? Can you describe it?

7. What advice do you have for young couples?

Raising Children

1. When did you first find out that you'd be a parent? How did you feel?

2. Can you describe the moment when you saw your child for the first time?

3. How many children do you have? When were they born? How old were you when they were born?

4. How has being a parent changed you?

5. What are your dreams for your children?

6. If you did not have children, what were the reasons?

7. Did you ever lose a child? How did you cope with the loss?

Separation, Divorce, Sexual Preference

1. If the relationship ended, describe the reasons. How long did the relationship last? If it ended in divorce, who initiated the divorce. Why? What were significant stresses? How did the divorce affect you financially and emotionally?

2. If you divorced with children, how did you and your ex-spouse handle child custody? Living arrangements for the children? Financial support for the children? How did it impact you?

3. Describe your experience as a mother/father, grandmother/grandfather.

4. If you are gay, when did you know your sexual nature? How did you feel about that realization?

5. When your parents, family or friends learned of your sexual nature, how did they react? If you have children, what do you tell them? If you have kept your sexual nature a secret, describe the impact of your decision.

6. Describe any difficulties you have experienced as a result of you sexual nature.

7. How has your attitude toward your relationships changed over time?

School and Employment

1. What did you think you were going to be when you grew up?

2. What did you want to be when you grew up?

3. When you entered the work force following higher education, did you experience any difficulties finding employment? If so, describe your experience.

4. Describe your various jobs. What did they entail? Did you enjoy your work? Why or why not? With a college education, what did you earn and how did your earnings compare with the pay of men in similar jobs?

5. Did you experience any difficulties in your employment? If so, describe the difficulties.

6. Did your career progress as you had hoped or expected? Why or why not?

7. What is your current occupation? Do you like it or not?

8. What aspects of your jobs/careers are different today?

9. How have you continued you education – formally and informally?

10. If you could do anything now, what would you do? Why?

11. Do you plan on retiring? If so, when?

12. What will you do after you retire?

Beliefs, Value Systems, Religion

1. What was your family's religious affiliation when you were a child? How religious was your family? How religious were you? Have your feelings about your religion or spirituality changed over time? What has been your source of spiritual support throughout your life?

2. Why and how were you punished as a child? How did you react? How has your personal experience with discipline or "justice" affected your attitudes about raising children or social justice?

3. Describe your philosophy of right and wrong and how you think it developed.

4. What is your religion?

5. What role does religion play in your life today?

6. Do you believe in God?

7. Do you believe in the after-life? If so, do you think you'll go to Heaven?

8. Have you experienced any miracles?

9. If you have children, what advice did/do you give them about their futures? Do you give the same advice to boys as to girls and boys? (for example, advice about morals, marriage, religion, education, work, etc.) Why or why not?

10. How has you belief/value system changed over time?

Traditions, Celebrations, and Trends

1. Did you participate in any special ceremonies in your early teenage years, such as a bar/bat mitzvah? Confirmation? Quinceanera? Debut? Describe the event and its impact on you.

2. How were these events different from the way they are celebrated today?

Aspirations and Dreams

1. When did you begin to think about what you would be when you grew up? What did you think you might or might not become?

2. What words of advice do you remember being given about your future? From whom? What influence did the advice have on you?

3. Did your dreams change throughout childhood?

Activities (Sports, Hobbies, Interests)

1. What activities do you enjoy for relaxation? How often do you do them? What are some of your favorite books or books influential in your life? What about movies, plays or other entertainment?

2. Throughout your life, what volunteer efforts have you undertaken for charities or nonprofit organizations? (for example, schools, Scouts or other youth groups, art groups, social service agencies, politics, church, and so on)

3. What influence has this service activity had on you?

4. What issues and organizations are most important to you? Have you contributed time or money to them?

5. What is your political affiliation, if any?

6. Do you vote? Have you ever participated in politics (supported a candidate, run for office, demonstrated, and so on)? Why or why not?

The Best of Times/The Worst of Times

1. What was the happiest moment of your life? The saddest?

2. Do you recall any incidents or issues in your adult life that have made a significant impact on you (accidents, hospitalization, moving, separation from a friend, divorce, remarriage, becoming a grandparent, sexuality, aging, career changes, death, or illness)?

3. What health issues have affected your life? Describe your illness.

4. Do you think about dying?

5. Are you scared?

6. How do you imagine your death?

7. Do you believe in an after-life?

8. Do you regret anything?

9. Do you look at your life differently now than before you were diagnosed?

10. Do you have any last wishes?

11. If you were to give advice to others, what would it be?

12. What have you learned from life? What are the most important things?

13. Has this illness changed you? What have you learned?

14. How do you want to be remembered?

15. How would you want to spend your last hours?

Family Heritage

1. What is your ethnic background?

2. Where is your mom's family from? Where is your dad's family from?

3. Have you ever been there? What was that experience like?

4. What traditions have been passed down in your family?

5. Who were your favorite relatives?

6. Do you remember any of the stories they used to tell you?

7. What are the classic family stories? Jokes? Songs?

8. Did your heritage/background create any special challenges for you?

Between You and Me

Ask your EP

1. Who do I remind you of among our family members or friends? In what ways do I remind you of that person?

2. What words would you use to describe me?

3. What about me reminds you of yourself?

4. What do you remember about me?

5. What is your favorite story or memory about me?

6. What, if anything, have you learned from me?

7. What do you think about me?

8. What about me are you most proud?

9. What do you wish for me?

10. What would you change about me if you could?

11. What advice would you give me now?

12. What do you love about me?

13. What do you want me to remember about you?

14. Is there something you want to tell me that you've not told me before?

15. What would you like me to tell you?

16. How would you want to spend your last hours with me?

Reflections

1. What individuals have had a significant impact on your life (for example, authors, bosses, friends, politicians, spiritual leaders)? When and how have they influenced you?

2. What advantages have you experienced regarding being married/single? What disadvantages?

3. If you could change your current circumstances, what would you do and why?

4. If you could change your past, would you? Why? How?

5. What is your philosophy of life? If you could change the world, what would you do?

6. How do you feel about your life's accomplishments? What accomplishments are you most proud of?

7. What do you feel most grateful for?

8. How would you like to be remembered?

9. Would you consider yourself a luminary? (A "notable" person; someone who is a source of light; or a "shining" example of someone who has others develop their capabilities as fully as possible.)

10. Who was the most important person in your life? Tell about him or her.

11. Who is the person who has been kindest to you in your life?

12. Can you remember a time when you felt alone?

13. What are the most important lessons you've learned in life?

14. What words of wisdom would you like to pass along?

15. What are you proudest of in your life?

16. What is your happiest memory?

17. How has your life been different than what you'd imagined?

18. Do you have any regrets?

19. What does your future hold?

20. Why do you think you are still here (alive)?

21. What or who is your source of inspiration?

22. What or who is it that gets you up and going every morning?

23. If you were to die suddenly this evening, what would you most regret having not told some-one?

24. Is there anything that you've never told but want to tell now?

APPENDIX I

Memoirs We Know and Love

Something of Myself (Rudyard Kipling)

Out of my Life and Thought (Albert Schweitzer)

Life So Far (Betty Freidan)

Josh: My Up and Down, In and Out Life (Joshua Logan)

Bubbles: A Self Portrait (Beverly Sills)

I Didn't Do It Alone (Art Linkletter)

A Backward Glance (Edith Wharton)

The World of Yesterday (Stefan Zweig)

The Summing Up (Somerset Maugham)

Angela's Ashes (Frank McCourt)

Living History (Hilary Rodham Clinton)

Tender at the Bone (Ruth Reichl)

BlackBerry Winter (Margaret Mead)

Personal History (Katherine Graham)

I Know Why the Caged Bird Sings (Maya Angelou)

Girl Interrupted (Susan Kaysen)

A Year in Provence (Peter Mayle)

Under the Tuscan Sun (Frances Mayes)

The House on Mango Street (Sandra Cisneros).

Ask your EP to add his or her favorite memoirs to the list.

Check out memoirs at Amazon.com. Search: memoirs about: (specific topics such as illness, divorce, childhood, etc.)

APPENDIX J

Alice Fern Sample Memoir

Life is Wonderful

By Alice Fern

Dedicated to my beautiful granddaughters, Carolina and Sofia

I lost my father my father, Herman, when I was just a toddler. He was the foreman of a fruit cannery in Ensenada, California. The company canned apricots, pears, and peaches and sent them north by ship to Los Angeles and San Francisco.

My father was kicked by a horse. Later, tragedy struck. He developed cancer and died when he was only thirty years old, leaving behind my mother and three siblings. My mother's family rescued us for a time. This postcard says it all:

Being the poor relations after my father's death was difficult for my family and for me especially. My mother was left with little means to raise her four young children.

In contrast, cousin Dorothy's family was well off. They lived on a ranch on Pico Avenue and raised vegetables and fruits. I especially liked the dewberries, a cross between blueberries and raspberries.

Dorothy, who was my age, was beautiful with long sausage curls. She had her own dressmaker and took music lessons. She even had a doll that looked like her. I was humble and ashamed of my situation. I had to wear hand-me-down clothes from Dorothy. My mother kept saying, "This too shall pass."   My Uncle Artie, who worked in the bank of London, tried to help me feel better about myself. He painted my bedroom blue and bought me an expensive hat and doll. My extended family enjoyed camping in Topanga Canyon, where there was a tent village. We took a stagecoach drawn by six horses to Topanga.

In nearby Venice, we rode on Italian-style gondolas. The gondoliers sang Italian songs. The canals were lit by electric globes that reflected in the water. I was determined never to feel like a poor relative again.

When I grew up, I met Vernon, a man sixteen years older than me. He was an organist at St. Augustine's Church and especially loved to play the music of Bach.

His family came to the United States from England. When the family moved to Hollywood, his father, Walter Charles, built a Victorian mansion. It had a turret and a long driveway that curved around the back of the house through an orchard.

Walter Charles was an organist and a builder of organs. He had a gigantic pipe organ in his house. The pipes ran up the wall by the staircase.

The dining room had a fancy rococo ceiling and the table was set with the best bone china. Every Saturday the family bought a big roast of beef and invited many guests for a sumptuous Sunday dinner. After the meal they played croquet on the front lawn, then had high tea. The meat lasted all week long and was cooked into hash and stews.

Looking back, I realize how much I was taken with Vernon's lifestyle—and the fact that he was so much older and sure of himself—perhaps a bit of a father-figure for me.

On August 22, 1919, Vernon and I were married in St. Augustine's. A bouquet of pink amaryllis lilies graced the end of each pew. Constructed in 1885, St. Augustine's Church was the second church built in Santa Monica. My extended family attended church here and had a family pew.

Many years later, my daughter, Winnie, was married here.

After our wedding Vernon and I lived with his parents in the Victorian mansion. A year later, we moved to a Craftsman-style house on 4th Street in Santa Monica.

I began to teach school and soon our daughter, Winifred, was born. Winnie was a delight. She was a happy baby who cooed and smiled—and stole your heart away. She was a contented baby who fit into our lifestyle with ease.

Winnie was cared for by my mother, whom she called "Donny." I remember how much Donny liked to wheel Winnie in her perambulator along the Santa Monica cliffs. Winnie loved sitting in cousin Dorothy's rocking chair as shown in the photograph.

Later, we traded the house in Santa Monica for a piece of land in the elegant Brentwood Heights neighborhood. We spent $8,000 building a large house with Greek columns along the front.

I worked at Brockton School in the Los Angles School District. I taught music and later became well-known throughout the city for the musical productions starring my students. Vernon worked for the Union Pacific Railroad as an accountant.

After we moved to the Brentwood Heights house, Donny continued to care for Winnie, because Vernon and I were busy working hard to pay for our big, expensive house. Vernon sometimes worked six days a week and I gave piano lessons after school.

I had a long and successful teaching career. I taught music and was well-known throughout Los Angeles for my musical productions starring my students. My Christmas performance of *Las Posadas* was especially popular.

Saturday was my favorite day of the week. Vernon usually worked only half day, and brought home fresh bread and butter from downtown Los Angeles.

The smell of freshly baked bread preceded his entrance and Winnie couldn't wait to run and greet him. We would spread a blanket in the back yard and have a lovely picnic of delicious treats—meat and cheese with tomatoes and avocados, followed by fresh fruit and cookies.

After lunch, we worked together in the garden. Winnie was especially fond of my mother's roses—the pink varietals. They became my favorite too.

I remember the moment that I learned of my mother's death. I had been looking at the borders of roses at our Brentwood house. I was thunderstruck by the news. Winnie was heartbroken, as was I.

She was a teen by then and hardly needed babysitting, but her fondness for Donny never wavered. I continued on, happy to have my music and teaching job to take my mind of the loss of my mother.

Winnie grew up and married and later moved to Mexico City with her husband. I traveled to Mexico during school vacations to visit my two lovely young granddaughters.

I've been lucky to have lived throughout southern California—in the coastal towns of Laguna Beach, Newport Beach, Santa Barbara, Ojai, Del Mar, and now La Jolla. I was delighted when Winnie moved back to Southern California and after Vernon's death, I moved in with my daughter and her family.

When I step out into my garden and the beauty takes my breath away. The fuchsia glistens with brilliance in the morning sun, their array of colors, red, purple, yellow, remind me of a rainbow after a storm. Of course, we haven't had a storm here in San Diego for months. We're in the driest season, so I have to take special care of my flowers.

Everyone seems to marvel at the tropical display I've created here on the front lawn. It's the crowning glory of my gardening experience.

Now as I tend my roses, I hear Carolyn practicing Bach on the piano and I smile. I feel lucky to have such a loving family and the beauty of my garden and music.

Alice's Secret to her Happy Life

"Music gives a soul to the universe, wings to the mind, flight to the imagination, and life to everything."
– Plato

Dear Grandma Alice,

I am so happy you are writing your life story. I'm so excited to read it and see all the old photos. I know it's hard work for you and I want you to know how important it is to me.

You've told me about your life in bits and pieces during our time together. But having it in writing so I can share it with my friends—and some day my children, is priceless.

You have been the best grandma. I love helping you plant your garden and watering and tending the roses. And I love when we sit at the piano together and play our favorite songs. If it weren't for you, I wouldn't have tried out for my school play—and gotten the lead role. So you have been wonderful to me—especially in building my confidence.

I am so lucky to you have you as my grandmother. I can't wait to read your story.

Much love,

Sofia

APPENDIX K

Beyond the Book: Resources for Memoir Partners

Check out 7Memories.com for numerous resources, including:

- Memoir-writing tips

- Partnering pages

- Life story basics

- Photo memoir basics

- Memoir prompts

- Complimentary feedback

- Editing services

- Contests and giveaways

- **Book: *7Memories: Write Your Memoir in 28 Days***

- **Online program: MemoirMagic™**

LIKE us on Facebook: Facebook.com/7memories4ever
FOLLOW US on Twitter: #7memories4ever

Get the digital templates file for entering your EP's memories directly on your computer. E-mail: Info@7Memories.com.

9 780998 681832